ETHIOPIA

Steven Gish & Winnie Thay & Zawiah Abdul Latif

 Marshall Cavendish
Benchmark

New York

PICTURE CREDITS
Cover photo: © Robert Harding World Imagery / Getty Images
alt.TYPE / Reuters: 31, 32, 34, 59 • Bridgeman Art Library: 20 • Corbis Inc.: 88, 103, 128 • Eising / Stockfood: 131 • Focus
Team: 6, 18, 36, 44, 52, 54, 57, 60, 76, 86, 94, 95 • Hulton-Deutsch: 19, 21 • Hutchison Library: 9, 10, 23, 24, 53, 55, 56, 73, 81,
90, 93, 121, 122 • Image Bank: 7, 64, 78, 109 • Bjorn Klingwall: 42, 58, 82, 84, 96, 97, 99, 101, 105, 106, 108, 126, 127
• Lonely Planet Images: 1, 4, 5, 8, 12, 14, 16, 28, 38, 43, 47, 48, 51, 62, 65, 70, 74, 79, 80, 100, 104, 112, 118, 120, 123, 124,
125, 129 • Seper, George / Stockfood: 130 • Bernard Sonneville: 13, 40, 66, 77, 85, 87, 89, 111, 115, 116 • Liba Taylor: 15, 61,
63, 68, 69

PRECEDING PAGE
Three young shepherds at the Simien Mountains National Park.

Editorial Director (U.S.): Michelle Bisson
Editors: Deborah Grahame, Mabelle Yeo, Ruth Wan
Copyreaders: Deborah Federhen, Daphne Hougham
Designers: Jailani Basari, Bernard Go Kwang Meng
Cover picture researcher: Connie Gardner
Picture researchers: Thomas Khoo, Joshua Ang

Marshall Cavendish Benchmark
99 White Plains Road
Tarrytown, NY 10591
Web site: www.marshallcavendish.us

Originated and designed by Times Editions
An imprint of Marshall Cavendish International (Asia) Private Limited
A member of Times Publishing Limited

All Internet sites were correct and accurate at the time of printing. All monetary figures in this publication are in U.S. dollars.

Library of Congress Cataloging-in-Publication Data
Gish, Steven, 1963–
  Ethiopia / Steven Gish & Winnie Thay & Zawiah Abdul Latif. — 2nd ed.
    p. cm. — (Cultures of the world)
  Summary: "Provides comprehensive information on the geography, history, wildlife, governmental structure, economy, cultural
    diversity, peoples, religion, and culture of Ethiopia"—Provided by publisher.
  Includes bibliographical references and index.
    ISBN-13: 978-0-7614-2025-5
    ISBN-10: 0-7614-2025-8
  1. Ethiopia—Juvenile literature. I. Thay, Winnie. II. Latif, Zawiah Abdul. III. Title.
DT373.G57 2007
963—dc22   2006020819

Printed in China

9 8 7 6 5 4 3 2 1

CONTENTS

INTRODUCTION   5

GEOGRAPHY   7
*Peaks and valleys • Lakes and rivers • A multitude
of climates • Flora • Fauna • A rich urban heritage*

HISTORY   17
*Early human ancestors • The kingdom of Axum
• The Zagwe dynasty • New contacts and conflicts
• Menelik II • The era of Haile Selassie • Military rule,
1974–91 • The Federal Democratic Republic of Ethiopia*

GOVERNMENT   29
*Political organizations and parties • National
security • Foreign relations • The judiciary*

ECONOMY   37
*Agriculture • Manufacturing • Mining • Energy
• Transportation*

ENVIRONMENT   45
*Environmental concerns • Protected areas
• Conservation efforts*

ETHIOPIANS   53
Population • Ethnic groups • Social stratification

LIFESTYLE   61
*Birth and childhood • Marriage • Death • Rural living
• Urban living • Ethiopian women • Schools and
students • Living with AIDS*

Two girls stand in the doorway of their home. Poverty plagues the majority of Ethiopians.

RELIGION   77
Christianity • Islam • Traditional beliefs • Ethiopia's Jews

LANGUAGE   87
*Amharic • Ge'ez • Writing systems • The challenges of
diversity • Language and education*

ARTS   95
*Literature and drama • Visual arts • Challenges facing
women artists • Arts and crafts • Song and dance*

LEISURE   105
*Popular sports • Sports unique to Ethiopia • Games people
play • Youth recreation*

FESTIVALS   113
*Ganna • Timkat • Enkutatash • Maskal • Kullubi
• Islamic holidays*

FOOD   121
*Cooking, Ethiopian style • Popular dishes • Beverages
• Dining out in Addis Ababa • Traditions and etiquette*

MAP OF ETHIOPIA   132

ABOUT THE ECONOMY   135

ABOUT THE CULTURE   137

TIME LINE   138

GLOSSARY   140

FURTHER INFORMATION   141

BIBLIOGRAPHY   142

INDEX   142

A shopper scrutinizes the craftmanship of a coffee pot on sale at a market in Axum.

INTRODUCTION

ETHIOPIA, WHOSE NAME is derived from the ancient Greek phrase for "land of the people with sunburned faces," is the oldest independent nation in Africa. It is a land rich in historical and cultural diversity. It is home to 74.8 million people, more than 100 different ethnic groups, 70 languages, and adherents of four major religions. Ethiopia's rugged landscape of grasslands, forests, lakes, and waterfalls may also have been home to one of our earliest ancestors 4 million years ago. Until 1974 Ethiopia was governed by one of the world's oldest monarchies. Contemporary Ethiopia is a country in transition. It went through a period of violent coups, famine, and ill-conceived policies in the 1980s. Although Ethiopia is still largely dependent on foreign aid, the adoption of the constitution of the Federal Republic of Ethiopia in 1994 saw political and economic situations finally stabilize, albeit in a slow but steady manner. Ethiopia today, although struggling to be economically independent, politically stable, and socially integrated, has the potential to reclaim the greatness of its past and compete in the world economy, for Ethiopia is a country of survivors.

GEOGRAPHY

ETHIOPIA IS LOCATED in the Horn of Africa, the part of the African continent that juts out into the Indian Ocean and lies just to the south of the Arabian Peninsula. Directly to the north of Ethiopia lies Eritrea, which gained its independence from Ethiopia in 1993. Bordering Ethiopia to the east is Djibouti; to the south and east, Somalia; to the south, Kenya; and to the west, Sudan. Ethiopia lies entirely between the equator and the Tropic of Cancer. Its territory spans 435,186 square miles (1.13 million square km), making it nearly three times larger than California.

Ethiopia is one of the most mountainous countries in Africa. It contains two highland regions separated by the Great Rift Valley, a vast low-lying area that divides the country roughly in half. Elevations in both highland regions can measure 7,500 feet (2,286 m) or higher. Ethiopia's rugged terrain makes regional transportation and communication difficult, but, historically, it has also protected the country from invaders.

Another key feature of Ethiopia's geography is the lack of reliable rainfall in several parts of the country. Precipitation is particularly scant in low-lying areas such as the Great Rift Valley, the Ogaden region in the southeast, and the Denakil Depression in the northeast. Droughts in these areas caused major famines in 1973 and 1984, with the latter one claiming more than a million lives. Similar dry spells are expected to torment the Ethiopian people in the future.

Above: **Ethiopia is situated in an area of intense geological activity, as evidenced by the many small volcanoes, hot springs, and gorges that punctuate its landscape. Several volcanoes lie in the Denakil Depression alone; seismic faults there also cause periodic earthquakes.**

Opposite: **Antelopes graze in the semiarid grasslands of Ethiopia. Ethiopia is home to an amazing array of landscapes.**

Ras Dejen Peak, located in the Simien Mountains, is the highest point in Ethiopia, soaring to a height of 15,158 feet (4,620 m).

A view of the Simien Mountains from a vantage point on Imet Gogo Mountain.

PEAKS AND VALLEYS

Elevation is the single most important factor defining Ethiopia's geography. It determines the climate, vegetation, soil composition, and settlement patterns of every region in the country.

Due to its mountainous terrain, Ethiopia is sometimes called "the roof of Africa." Its two major highland regions dominate the western and south central portions of the country. Rising to the west of the Great Rift Valley is the Amhara Plateau, home to the Simien and Choke mountain ranges.

The elevation of these western highlands generally ranges from 7,800 to 12,000 feet (2,377 to 3,658 m) above sea level. The Somali Plateau lies to the east of the Great Rift Valley and contains the Ahmar and Mendebo mountains. Several peaks in the Mendebo Mountains rise above 13,000 feet (3,962 m).

Valleys, deserts, and grasslands also contribute to the country's varied landscape. The Great Rift Valley cuts through much of eastern Africa and extends all the way to Mozambique in southern Africa. In Ethiopia, the Great Rift Valley ranges from 25 to 40 miles wide (40 to 64 km). The northern portion of the valley contains the Denakil Depression, a desert area that lies 380 feet (116 m) below sea level. The valley's southwestern portion is dotted by a chain of freshwater and salt lakes.

The **Blue Nile flows south from Lake Tana and is the country's longest river, flowing for 850 miles (1,368 km) into neighboring Sudan.**

LAKES AND RIVERS

The chain of lakes in the Great Rift Valley includes lakes Abaya, Abiata, Koka, Langano, Shala, Shamo, and Zwai. Ethiopia's largest lake is Lake Tana, which lies in the northern part of the country. This freshwater lake is the source of the Blue Nile River. The Blue Nile is known to many Ethiopians as the Abbai River.

Other smaller rivers in Ethiopia include the Awash, Baro, Shebelle, and Tekeze. The government has built dams on the Awash River to generate hydroelectric power and to provide irrigation for commercial farms. Most of Ethiopia's rivers originate in highland areas and flow outward through deep gorges. This has created a series of rapids and waterfalls that, though scenic, make navigation on the rivers virtually impossible. Of all of Ethiopia's rivers, only the Awash and Baro rivers are navigable.

A MULTITUDE OF CLIMATES

Ethiopia's varied topography and its location in Africa's tropical zone have resulted in diverse rainfall and temperature patterns. Determined to a large extent by elevation, the country's climate has three environmental zones—cool, temperate, and hot.

The highlands experience moderate to cool temperatures ranging from near-freezing to 62°F (17°C), with March, April, and May being the warmest months. Lower areas of the plateau, between 4,920 to 7,872 feet (1,500 to 2,400 m) in elevation, constitute the temperate zone, where daily highs range from 59°F to 72°F (15°C to 22°C). The hospitable climate of the highland regions helps explain why they are home to the majority of Ethiopia's population. Situated in the highlands is Addis Ababa, Ethiopia's capital and largest city.

The Denakil Depression is Ethiopia's hottest region. The highest temperature ever recorded there was 120°F (49°C).

The Ethiopian lowlands, located chiefly in the north central and eastern portions of the country, constitute the country's hottest parts. Although the average daytime temperature is about 81°F (27°C), mid-year readings can soar from 86°F (30°C) to 120°F (49°C) in the arid and semiarid areas. Population density in the lowlands is significantly lower than it is on the plateaus.

ETHIOPIA'S CLIMATIC ZONES

- **Alpine:** *kur* **(kuhr)**
  Location: Ethiopia's highest elevations
  Elevation: Over 10,800 feet (3,292 m)
  Temperatures: Below 50°F (10°C)
  Features of interest: Regular frost; snow on highest mountain peaks. Unsuitable for agriculture.
- **Cool zone:** *dega* **(DEH-ga)**
  Location: Chiefly northwestern (Amhara) plateau
  Elevation: 7,500–10,800 feet (2,286–3,292 m)
  Temperatures: 34°F–61°F (1°C–16°C)
  Features of interest: Warmest months are March to May. Light frost is common at night in the higher elevations.
- **Temperate zone:** *weina dega* **(WAY-nuh DEH-ga)**
  Location: Lower areas of Amhara and Somali plateaus
  Elevation: 4,900–7,500 feet (1,493–2,286 m)
  Temperatures: 59°F–72°F (15°C–22°C)
- **Hot zone:** *kolla* **(KOH-la)**
  Location: Eastern Ogaden, valleys of the Blue Nile and Tekeze rivers, areas along Kenyan and Sudanese borders
  Elevation: 1,600–4,900 feet (488–1,493 m)
  Temperatures: Average daytime temperature is 81°F (27°C)
  Features of interest: The river valleys receive more rainfall than the border areas.
- **Semidesert:** *bereha* **(ber-eh-HAH)**
  Location: Denakil Depression and other scattered, low-lying regions of Ethiopia
  Elevation: Below 1,600 feet (488 m)
  Temperatures: 86°F–120°F (30°C–49°C)
  Features of interest: Arid; unsuitable for agriculture

The rainy season is regarded as winter, even though it falls during the summer months, because cloud cover and rains reduce the temperature. The high plateau often gets heavy hailstorms during the rainy season.

Precipitation is influenced by both elevation and season. Ethiopia receives most of its precipitation during the rainy season, which lasts from June to September. The highlands generally receive at least 39 inches (99 cm) of rainfall per year. Southwestern Ethiopia is the most well-watered part of the country, receiving an average of 56 inches (142 cm) of rainfall per year.

Geladas, related to baboons, inhabit the mountains of southern Ethiopia, living on the cliffs of rocky ravines.

The lowlands are much drier than the highlands and usually receive less than 19.5 inches (50 cm) of rain per year. Rainfall is particularly scant in the Great Rift Valley and the Ogaden region. Drier still is the Denakil Depression, which receives only a few inches of precipitation annually. In bad years there is no rain at all. The Ethiopian drought of 1984 claimed the lives of nearly 1 million people and put 8 million more on the brink of starvation. Pictures of malnourished Ethiopian children and crowded refugee camps were broadcast all over the world and triggered a massive international relief effort.

FLORA

The amount of rainfall (or lack thereof) in Ethiopia's various regions greatly affects the variety and quantity of plant life. In the driest areas, only occasional bushes and thorn scrub are found. In areas classified as semiarid, grasslands are common, as are acacia trees and sansevieria (snake plants). The cooler and wetter highlands are home to eucalyptus, yellowwood trees, and juniper. Southwestern Ethiopia's combination of low elevation and high rainfall has produced rain forests thick with trees, ferns, and undergrowth. This unique highland ecology provided ample opportunities for Ethiopia's ancient farmers to experiment with a wide variety of crops. It is no surprise then that ancient Ethiopia was the original site of the cultivation of many food crops, including teff, which is

an iron-rich grain from which the bread *injera* (in-JAIR-ah) is made, and probably coffee. Today some of Ethiopia's world-famous coffee grows wild in these southwestern rain forests.

FAUNA

Ethiopia is home to an extraordinarily wide range of wildlife that in some cases have been diminished to near extinction. Foxes, jackals, wild dogs, and hyenas are commonly found throughout the country. Varieties of antelopes and monkeys are abundant in the lowlands. Elephants, giraffes, leopards, lions, rhinoceroses, and wild buffalo are rarities. Unique to Ethiopia and among the most endangered is the Walia ibex, a rare species of mountain goat that is found in the Simien Mountains. The country's lakes and rivers host crocodiles, hippopotamuses, and various other reptiles and species of fish. The Great Rift Valley is known for its bird life, which includes eagles, flamingos, and hawks. Other birds native to Ethiopia include the egret, hornbill, ibis, ostrich, pelican, stork, and vulture.

Describing the Merkato (the central market) in Addis Ababa, one early-20th century traveler wrote, "In the palpitating life and varied scenes of the market, one might see more of the people and their ways of life in one morning than in a week's wandering about the capital."

A RICH URBAN HERITAGE

Although only 15 percent of Ethiopians live in urban areas, the cities they inhabit have long histories and compelling points of interest. Addis Ababa, the capital, has been described as a "cultural jigsaw puzzle" because of its rich mixture of peoples and lifestyles. It is also one of the largest inland cities in Africa. In 2005 the capital had an estimated population of about 3 million. The city is situated in the highlands at an altitude of 8,000 feet (2,438 m) and enjoys a temperate climate.

Besides serving as Ethiopia's capital, Addis Ababa is an important diplomatic center for the African continent. It is home to approximately 97 foreign embassies and hosts international agencies such as the World Health Organization (WHO) and the United Nations Children's Fund (UNICEF). The city also serves as the headquarters for the African Union (formerly known as the Organization of African Unity, or OAU).

Ethiopia's second largest city is Dire Dawa, which had a population of 398,000 in 2005. Dire Dawa lies between Addis Ababa and the coast and serves as an important rail terminus. In addition to Addis Ababa and Dire Dawa, Ethiopia's other important centers of trade and industries are Awassa, Gonder, Dessie, Nazareth, Jimma, Harrar, Bahir Dar, Mekele, Debre Markos, and Nekemite.

ADDIS ABABA

Modern Addis Ababa began to take shape in 1889, when the Ethiopian monarch Menelik II started building a palace near the ruins of the 16th-century capital at Entoto. Menelik's Queen Taytu marveled at the flowering mimosa trees in the area, and thus the town was named Addis Ababa, meaning "new flower." It officially became Ethiopia's capital in 1896. Other important dates for Addis Ababa are 1958, when the city became the first  headquarters of the United Nations (UN) Economic Commission for Africa, and 1963, when it hosted the African Heads of State Conference at which the OAU Charter was signed.

Among the many points of interest in Addis Ababa, two in particular stand out. One is the Giorgis Cathedral, also known as Saint George's Cathedral, which was built in 1896 to commemorate Ethiopia's victory over the Italians at the Battle of Adwa. Giorgis Cathedral features impressive stained glass created by Ethiopian artist Afewerk Tekle. Another urban wonder is the Merkato, one of Africa's largest open-air markets. Here, a dazzling array of goods is displayed for sale, including vegetables, spices, clothing, and jewelry. As it draws Ethiopians from far beyond the capital, the Merkato has been described as a melting pot for the country's different languages and cultures.

Two cities of particular historical significance are Axum and Gondar. Axum, located in northern Ethiopia near the Eritrean border, was the capital of ancient Ethiopia. Two thousand years ago, this holy city was on par with the great urban centers of Nubia, Egypt, and Greece. Axum is home to the Saint Mary of Zion Church, built in the 16th and 17th centuries and considered to be the holiest shrine in Ethiopia. Axum is also noted for its huge granite sculptures known as obelisks, some of which were over 75 feet (23 m) tall. Most of them have since fallen to the ground. Gondar, located just north of Lake Tana, served as the Ethiopian capital between 1632 and 1868. Today some of its surviving castles are used as government office buildings.

HISTORY

THERE IS MUCH that makes the history of Ethiopia unique. First, and perhaps most significant, is that Ethiopia was home to the earliest-known human ancestors. A team of anthropologists discovered skeletal remains of humanlike beings that date back over 5 million years. Second, Ethiopia embraced an early form of Christianity over 1,000 years before European missionaries spread this religion throughout the rest of Africa. Third, Ethiopia was one of only two African countries to remain independent during the era of European colonization beginning in the late 19th century (the other country was Liberia in West Africa). Finally, Ethiopia was involved in modern Africa's longest war, the Eritrean conflict, which lasted from 1962 to 1991.

EARLY HUMAN ANCESTORS

In November 1994 paleoanthropologists Tim White and his colleagues, Gen Suwa and Berhane Asfaw, made a once-in-a-lifetime discovery. While examining a hillside near Aramis on Ethiopia's Awash River, the researchers uncovered a group of humanlike hand bones that were approximately 4.4 to 4.5 million years old. Soon other anthropologists working in the area found additional bones from the same skeleton and reconstructed almost the entire skeleton. In January 1995 the scientists announced their discovery to the world, naming it *Australopithecus ramidus*. Seven months later its name was changed to *Ardipithecus ramidus*. In 2001 Yohannes Haile Selassie, an Ethiopian scientist trained in the United States, discovered 5.2 million-year-old bones related to the *Ardipithecus ramidus* family 15.5 miles (25 km) from Aramis. Although further research needs to be done to ascertain the origins of these fossils, such finds are of great significance in tracing our true human origins.

Opposite: **The stelae (rectangular stone monuments) of Tiya date back to prehistoric times. Due to its cultural significance, it has been recognized as a World Heritage Site by UNESCO.**

Skeletal remains of a female hominid known affectionately as "Lucy" were discovered in 1974 in Ethiopia. This skeleton was approximately 3.1 million years old and, remarkably, scientists found 40 percent of her fossil bones, including a jaw, an arm bone, a thigh bone, ribs, and vertebrae. Ethiopians call the Lucy skeleton "Dinkenesh," which means "she is wonderful."

Archaeological evidence found in Ethiopia attests to the early hominid activity in the region. This evidence includes stone hand tools, sharp cutting instruments, and drawings found in limestone caves located near Dire Dawa. By approximately 5000 B.C., hunters and gatherers had established communities on the Ethiopian highlands. Grain cultivation and animal husbandry appeared in the northwest highlands some time before 2000 B.C.

THE KINGDOM OF AXUM

Modern Ethiopia traces its origins to the great kingdom of Axum, one of Africa's most important cultural and trading centers during the first half of the first millennium A.D. Migrants from southern Arabia laid the foundations of the kingdom by bringing their language and stone-building

The primary language of the Axumite kingdom was Ge'ez, a vernacular that gave rise to Amharic in the Middle Ages.

Merchants from Axum traded not only there, but also with inhabitants of what is now Sudan, the Nile River valley, the Red Sea coast, southern Arabia, and the eastern Mediterranean. Testifying to Axum's wealth were the many temples, castles, and obelisks constructed in this era, some of which survive to this day.

THE ORIGINS OF THE ETHIOPIAN MONARCHY

Many of the legends surrounding the Ethiopian ruling dynasty originated in the 14th century. In this period, six scribes from the region of Tigray in north Ethiopia proclaimed that the country's monarchy was descended from the Queen of Sheba and King Solomon in order to infuse the monarchy with a glorious past and create a proud heritage for the Ethiopian kingdom. Whether or not the scribes' proclamation was completely true puzzles historians to this day.

The legend claims that in the 10th century B.C., the Queen of Sheba visited King Solomon in Jerusalem, who became her mentor in the art of royal statecraft. The queen eventually converted to Judaism and became romantically involved with King Solomon. She then returned to Ethiopia and bore a son, Menelik I, who was declared king of that country by his father, King Solomon.

After Menelik's death, those claiming to be his descendants ruled the kingdom of Axum for centuries. The Zagwe dynasty temporarily interrupted the Solomonic line, but by the 13th century, a new king claiming to be one of Menelik's descendants gained the throne. Thus, the Solomonic dynasty was restored, even though some of Menelik's successors may not have been his direct descendants. The dynasty would continue to rule Ethiopia until Emperor Haile Selassie's ouster in 1974.

traditions to the northeastern African coast beginning around 1000 B.C. The Axumite kingdom began to take shape in the first century A.D. in the north and central portions of present-day Ethiopia. The kingdom became a thriving trading center in which merchants exchanged gold and ivory for cloth, glassware, tools, and other materials.

Christianity became the state religion of the Axumite kingdom during King Ezanas's rule in the fourth century. The establishment of the Ethiopian Orthodox Church—heavily influenced by the Coptic Church in

An Ethiopian painting shows the Battle of Adwa. This Ethiopian victory secured Ethiopia's independence.

Egypt—would entrench the Christian tradition in Ethiopia for centuries to come. But other religious traditions also gained a foothold in Ethiopia. Judaism began spreading in the region in the early sixth century, and Islam started to gain converts along the coast two centuries later. The rise of Islam in the 10th and 11th centuries led to the decline of Axum, as Christians retreated to the highlands and lost their preeminence in the kingdom's outlying regions.

THE ZAGWE DYNASTY

The Zagwe dynasty, which ruled Ethiopia in the 12th and 13th centuries, temporarily broke the Solomonic hold on the monarchy. This period is seen as an era of great artistic achievement, during which impressive rock churches were carved and dedicated to the glory of God.

NEW CONTACTS AND CONFLICTS

According to the *Kebre Nagast*, also known as the *Book of the Glory of Kings*, the Solomonic dynasty was restored around 1270. During the next two centuries, the new regime consolidated its authority and encouraged the spread of the Amharic language and Orthodox Christianity throughout the Ethiopian highlands.

By the late 15th century, however, incursions by outsiders threatened to destabilize the established order. Around this time a Portuguese contingent

20

traveled to Ethiopia in hopes of finding Christian allies to help them curb the growing Islamic presence in the region. When Muslims launched an attack against Ethiopia in 1527, the Ethiopians appealed to the Portuguese for aid. The combined Ethiopian-Portuguese forces turned back the Muslim invaders. In this era, the Ethiopians still viewed the Europeans as allies despite their rebuffing Portuguese attempts to spread Roman Catholicism in their country.

Contacts between Ethiopia and Europe were relatively infrequent between the mid-17th and late-18th centuries. The situation changed dramatically in the 19th century. In this era, Italy, Britain, and France cast their eyes on Ethiopia. Three Ethiopian emperors stood in the way of the European colonial advance: Tewodros II (1855–68), Yohannis IV (1872–89), and Menelik II (1889–1913). During the Napier expedition of 1867–68, a British force of 3,000 troops was sent to Ethiopia to secure the release of British officials held by Emperor Tewodros II. As the British troops advanced, Tewodros committed suicide to avoid capture. The British soon withdrew from Ethiopia, but the Italians seemed more anxious to stay. They acquired the ports of Aseb in 1869 and Massawa in 1885 before being expelled by Ethiopian forces.

Emperor Menelik II.

MENELIK II

Emperor Menelik II faced still greater threats to Ethiopia's sovereignty. Shortly after he came to power in 1889, Menelik signed a treaty allowing the Italians to occupy Asmara, but renounced it in 1893 when Italy sought to extend its authority to Ethiopia as a whole. When the Italians began moving southward into Ethiopian territory, Menelik distributed weapons obtained from France and Russia, assembled a national army from Ethiopia's diverse ethnic groups, and readied his troops for battle. On March 1, 1896, the Ethiopian army confronted the Italians at the Battle of Adwa and scored a decisive victory. The peace treaty signed later that year preserved Ethiopia's independence during the height of Europe's scramble for Africa. The kingdom emerged from its victory with considerable prestige, both in Africa and Europe, although Eritrea remained under Italian control. Menelik also consolidated the monarchy's control over the non-Christian populations in the east and south, creating the boundaries of modern Ethiopia.

THE ERA OF HAILE SELASSIE

Haile Selassie I ruled Ethiopia between 1930 and 1974 and is considered one of 20th-century Africa's most important leaders; his reforms are said to have altered the course of Ethiopia's history. During Haile Selassie's reign, Ethiopia began to modernize its political and economic system, despite facing threats of famine, foreign occupation, and ethnic division.

Haile Selassie's first challenge was to preserve Ethiopian independence in the face of renewed Italian aggression. In October 1935, Italy invaded Ethiopia in an attempt to avenge its loss at Adwa 39 years earlier. Italian troops entered Addis Ababa on May 5, 1936, and formally annexed Ethiopia four days later. The emperor went into exile in Britain and appealed to the League of Nations to take strong action against the Italians, but little was done initially. Fortunately for Ethiopia, the Italian occupation did not last. With the help of the British, Haile Selassie organized an Ethiopian resistance force in neighboring Sudan and led an invasion into Ethiopia in January 1941.

Born in 1892 into an Amharic family related to Menelik II, Haile Selassie was originally known as Ras Tafari. Influential Christian chieftains declared him heir to the throne in 1916. In 1930 he was crowned emperor, and took the name Haile Selassie I, which means "Lion of Judah."

The emperor's troops reentered Addis Ababa on May 5, 1941, exactly five years after the Italian conquest. Following Italy's surrender on May 20, 1941, Haile Selassie was reestablished as emperor.

Haile Selassie initiated important reforms between the 1940s and 1960s. He encouraged the development of a secular educational system; attracted Western economic and technical assistance; approved a new constitution in 1955, which provided for parliamentary elections; curbed the power of the aristocracy and the church; and declared Amharic the official language of Ethiopia. He also played an active role in the establishment of the Organization of African Unity (OAU), now known as the African Union, which first met in Addis Ababa in 1963. Subsequently the city became the site of the African Union's headquarters.

Internal pressures posed serious problems for Haile Selassie's government, particularly from the 1960s onward, starting with an unsuccessful December 1960 coup d'état. Several groups, impatient with Selassie's seeming inability to effect social and political reform, tried to overthrow his government while he was abroad. In 1962 Eritreans began their long armed struggle against Ethiopian rule and students clashed with police during demonstrations for Eritrean independence

THE STRUGGLE FOR ERITREA

Tension between Ethiopia and Eritrea began to intensify shortly after World War II. Following the war, the United Nations nullified Italian control over Eritrea and placed it under the Ethiopian crown as an autonomous territory. In 1962 Haile Selassie annexed Eritrea as a province of Ethiopia. Eritreans quickly established the Eritrean Liberation Front to spearhead their bid for independence. Few realized that 30 years of bitter struggle lay ahead.

After eight years of sporadic guerrilla warfare, a new Marxist group, the Eritrean People's Liberation Front (EPLF), gained control over the rebel forces in Eritrea and fought a long war to end Ethiopian control, ultimately leading to independence on May 24, 1993.

At the time of Eritrea's independence, the border between the two countries was undefined and several areas, including the town of Badme, were subject to dispute. On May 6, 1998, armed clashes over the border led to the Eritrean-Ethiopian War that lasted until June 2000, when a peace treaty was signed in Algeria. A fragile truce was held, but Ethiopia's rejection of the independent arbitration commission's decision to award the disputed town of Badme and other territories to Eritrea resulted in a prolonged stalemate on demarcating the frontier. In 2006 Eritrea, increasingly frustrated by Ethiopia's failure to cede Badme, sent its troops to a demilitarized buffer zone between the two countries. The United Nations was critical of Eritrea's decision and said that the operation constituted "a major breach of the ceasefire."

and for land and educational reform in the 1960s and 1970s. To make matters worse, a major famine broke out in the Tigray and Welo provinces between 1972 and 1974, causing the deaths of approximately 200,000 Ethiopians. By 1974 groups of students, workers, and soldiers were demanding the dismissal of Haile Selassie's cabinet. The emperor, then aged 82, was unable to stem the rising tide of discontent. On September 12, 1974, a group of army officers deposed Haile Selassie and set up a new military government. The 3,000-year-old Ethiopian monarchy had finally come to an end.

Haile Selassie died in Ethiopia in August 1975 while under house arrest. He was allegedly killed by backers of the new military government.

MILITARY RULE, 1974–91

With the overthrow of Haile Selassie, the Ethiopian monarchy was abolished and replaced by a military regime, and the country's economic orientation shifted from capitalism to Marxism. The new regime that took power in mid-1974 was known as the Derg (durg), an Amharic word meaning "committee." The Derg was composed of 120 military officers and was led by an Eritrean general, Aman Andom. During its first few months in power, the regime instituted press censorship, curtailed civil rights, and executed 60 former imperial officials. Next, the regime suspended the constitution and dissolved parliament.

In December 1974 the government announced the creation of a one-party state and began to restructure the Ethiopian economy along socialist lines. Officials drew up plans for collective farms, confiscated private property, and nationalized many foreign-owned corporations. Many of those who opposed the regime—including students, church leaders, and members of the former government—were imprisoned, forced into exile, or killed.

The government's use of famine as a weapon in 1985 caused untold misery among millions of Ethiopians, as did its efforts to forcibly resettle rural communities.

The rise of Mengistu Haile Mariam ushered in even more violence. The military government had launched a major new effort to wipe out its opponents in 1976, and Mengistu intensified the campaign when he came to power in 1977. During the Red Terror of 1976–78, over 100,000 Ethiopians are believed to have been killed by the military authorities. In May 1977 the government executed 500 students. Ethiopians who survived the fearful days and nights of the Red Terror recall seeing new victims of the government's campaign of terror almost every day.

The Mengistu government received significant economic and military assistance from the Soviet Union beginning in the late 1970s, and thus initially maintained a firm grip on power. But escalating crises at home began to cripple the regime by the 1980s. Insurgencies in Eritrea, Tigray, and Ogaden challenged the Ethiopian military machine more seriously than ever before. In 1983 a massive famine broke out in Ethiopia, claiming the lives of at least 300,000 people by 1985. Although a major international relief effort was launched to aid famine victims, these efforts were hindered by the government's policy of blocking food deliveries to regions it considered politically hostile.

By the mid- to late 1980s opposition to the Mengistu regime began to intensify, especially among leftist intellectuals, students, and workers. Representatives of various rebel groups soon united to form the Ethiopian

People's Revolutionary Democratic Front (EPRDF). The EPRDF called for the removal of Mengistu and the establishment of a democratic government in Addis Ababa. It stepped up the armed struggle against Mengistu's forces in the late 1980s.

From 1989 to 1990 the breakup of the Soviet Union resulted in the collapse of Ethiopia's overseas support network; sources of much-needed economic aid could no longer be counted on. After rebel troops began closing in on Addis Ababa in May 1991, Mengistu fled to Zimbabwe and left his government to collapse. On May 28, 1991, the EPRDF took control of the capital and declared Meles Zenawi the country's interim president.

THE FEDERAL DEMOCRATIC REPUBLIC OF ETHIOPIA

Following the overthrow of the military junta in 1991, political and economic conditions began to stabilize. Once in power, Zenawi and his backers announced their support for a federal form of government in order to accommodate the needs of Ethiopia's many ethnic groups. The government organized local and regional elections in 1992 and 1993 and accepted the coming of independence to Eritrea. In 1994 the constitution of the Federal Democratic Republic of Ethiopia was adopted, leading to the nation's first multiparty elections the following year. Most opposition parties chose to boycott these elections, ensuring a landslide victory for the EPRDF.

In 2000 Zenawi's government was reelected. In 2005 his ruling party again won a bitterly contested election, during which the opposition accused the ruling front of election fraud and demonstrations by the public led to the death of some protesters and the arrests of dozens more.

Many Ethiopians depend on food aid from abroad. In 2004 the government began a drive to move more than 2 million people away from the arid highlands of the east, proposing that this resettlement would reduce food shortages.

27

GOVERNMENT

THE FEDERAL DEMOCRATIC REPUBLIC of Ethiopia (FDRE) was established in 1995 after a new constitution was ratified in December 1994. The constitution provided autonomy to ethnically based regions while reserving defense, foreign affairs, and constitutional issues for the federal government.

The FDRE comprises the federal government, nine member states with self-determining powers, and two administrative cities—Addis Ababa and Dire Dawa. Each member state is governed by a State Council that answers to the people. The State Council is the highest authority in the state and has legislative power on matters falling under its jurisdiction. It also elects representatives to the House of the Federation, one of the two houses of parliament. The State Council can also hold elections to have representatives elected directly by the people of the state.

The House of People's Representatives is the other house of parliament and holds the highest authority of the federal government. The house is responsible to the Ethiopian people and has legislative power in all matters assigned to federal jurisdiction by the constitution. The political party or coalition of political parties with the greatest number of seats in the House of People's Representatives forms and leads the government of the FDRE. The EPRDF has been in power since 1995.

The head of state of the FDRE is the president, currently Girma Wolde Giorgis, incumbent since 2001. The president is nominated by the House of the People's Representatives and is elected if his candidacy is approved by a two-third majority vote at a joint session of the two houses of parliament. The term of the president is six years and no one can be elected president for more than two terms.

The highest executive power of the federal government is vested in the prime minister and his council of ministers, who in turn are accountable

Opposite: **A monument in Addis Ababa dedicated to Karl Marx, a philosopher whose ideas formed the foundation of Communism and Socialism. After overthrowing Emperor Selassie, the Derg tried to transform Ethiopia into a socialist country.**

Upon final ratification of the new constitution, Ethiopia's official name became the Federal Democratic Republic of Ethiopia.

to the House of the People's Representatives. The prime minister is the chief executive and chairman of the council of ministers and the commander in chief of the country's armed forces. Meles Zenawi has held this position since 1995.

POLITICAL ORGANIZATIONS AND PARTIES

The EPRDF dominates Ethiopian political life. Established in 1989 by the Tigray People's Liberation Front (TPLF), the EPRDF was originally an alliance of insurgent organizations seeking regional autonomy for the country's many ethnic groups. It defeated the Mengistu regime in 1991 after years of armed struggle. Although the TPLF is the dominant organization within the governing EPRDF, two other organizations form part of the coalition: the Tigray-based Amhara National Democratic Movement and the Shewa-based Oromo People's Democratic Organization. Meles Zenawi has led the EPRDF since its formation.

There are about 100 other political parties in Ethiopia, most of which are organized along ethnic lines. Political parties that were influential in the mid-1990s when the EPRDF came into power included the Council of Alternative Forces for Peace and Democracy in Ethiopia and the Coalition of Ethiopian Democratic Forces. These opposition parties opposed the ruling EPRDF's plan to devolve power to ethnically based regions and favored the creation of a strong central government to preserve Ethiopian unity. Others like the Oromo Liberation Front and the Ogaden National Liberation Front sought self-determination for their own ethnic peoples.

Today, the EPRDF's two main opponents are the Coalition for Unity and Democracy (CUD) and the United Ethiopian Democratic Forces (UEDF), both of which are coalition parties. During the May 2005 elections early results from the polls showed that the opposition was headed for a decisive victory. However, the National Electoral Board, which was appointed by the prime minister, stopped tabulating the votes for several days, and when counting resumed, the EPRDF claimed to have won 327 of the 547 seats and declared itself the winner. The CUD and UEDF accused the ruling front of electoral fraud and vote rigging in 299 constituencies. While the allegations were being investigated and the release of the election results placed on hold, a group of students demonstrated against the alleged discrepancies despite a ban on protests imposed by the government. As a result of rioting, 26 people were killed in Addis Ababa on June 8, 2005, and hundreds of others were arrested.

Student protestors in Addis Ababa confront Ethiopian police in the aftermath of the elections of 2006.

On September 5, 2005, the National Electoral Board released the final election results confirming EPRDF's win. The opposition, refusing to accept the results, called for a general strike and boycott of the new parliament. Again, in an effort to contain the protests, 42 people were killed in the capital city and thousands were arrested in early November. As of February 2006, six hundred remained in custody facing trial. Under international pressure the Ethiopian government passed a resolution to establish an independent commission to investigate the incidents of June and November 2005.

NATIONAL SECURITY

Ethiopia's military comprises only ground and air forces. When Eritrea gained independence in 1993, Ethiopia became a landlocked country and its small navy was ceded to Eritrea.

Ethiopian soldiers on the march.

Dominated by officers associated with the TPLF, a former guerrilla army, the Ethiopian National Defence Force (ENDF), is transforming from a militia force to a national body. Ranks and conventional units were adopted in 1996. With assistance from the United States, Ethiopia plans to restructure the ENDF into three military districts, each with its own corps, under the command of army headquarters in Addis Ababa.

There are army bases throughout the country including in the capital, Dire Dawa, Gondar, Gore, Jijiga, Bahir Dar, and Debre Zeyit. The defense budget for 2005 was $296 million, or 3.4 percent of the country's gross domestic product (GDP).

Despite the fragile truce established in December 2000, the major threat to Ethiopia's national security continues to be the unresolved border dispute with neighboring Eritrea. Although both nations can ill afford—both financially and politically—to rekindle the conflict, tensions remain high between them. The UN Mission in Ethiopia and Eritrea, fearing renewed clashes, has stationed troops on the Eritrean side of the border to maintain the brittle peace; but as of May 2006, it is planning to reduce its troops from 3,000 to 1,500, due to the prolonged failure to break the deadlock between the two countries.

HUMAN RIGHTS CONCERNS

Both international observers and Ethiopians themselves have expressed concerns over the Ethiopian government's poor human rights record. According to the U.S. Department of State's human rights report for 2004, the aftermath of the 2005 parliamentary elections clearly demonstrates the patterns of violence, human rights abuse, and political repression that are entrenched in the governance of much of the country. Heavy-handed efforts to curb press freedoms and suppress political dissent are two major areas of particular concern.

Although fewer journalists were arrested, detained, or punished in 2004 than in past years, the government nevertheless continues to restrict the freedom of the press. In 2003 the only independent media organization in the nation, the Ethiopian Free Journalists Association, was suspended for failure to comply with the state's onerous regulations.

In other cases, government officials and security forces selectively enforce harsh penalties such as imprisonment, seizure of property, and sustained harassment to silence their political opponents and even ordinary citizens. In December 2003, Ethiopian military forces were accused of human rights abuses in Anuak, the remote southwestern region of Gambella. Military personnel allegedly joined civilian mobs in rioting and murdering about 424 Anuak civilians. In the following months, they murdered, raped, tortured, and arbitrarily imprisoned local citizens, and destroyed entire Anuak villages throughout the region. A government-sponsored Commission of Inquiry asked to investigate the violence took no action, despite reports of abuses emerging from the Gambella region as recently as 2005. There are two local human rights organizations in Ethiopia—the Ethiopian Human Rights Council (EHRCO) and the Human Rights League. Both are often subjected to harassment and intimidation by local officials and security force members. Established in 1992, EHRCO has publicly criticized the authorities for detaining individuals without charge, dismissing government employees for political reasons, and for causing the "disappearance" of government opponents. In June 2005 three EHRCO investigators were arrested and taken to military detention camps because of their efforts to document the human toll of the government's postelection crackdown. All three were subsequently released but were threatened with future criminal proceedings. The Human Rights League reopened its offices in March 2005 after winning a protracted court battle against government efforts to ban its operations.

Ethnic Somalis in southeastern Ethiopia are still fighting for independence and continue to receive assistance from a Somali-backed guerrilla force.

The prime minister of Ethiopia, Meles Zenawi, holds talks on the "war on terror" with President George Bush at the White House in 2002.

FOREIGN RELATIONS

Ethiopia maintains formal diplomatic relations with approximately 70 countries, including 30 African nations. The country participates in major international treaties on the environment and chemical and biological weapons and is a member of organizations for international cooperation such as the International Criminal Police Organization, the International Federation of Red Cross and Red Crescent Societies, the United Nations, the World Trade Organization, and the International Monetary Fund. Under Haile Selassie I, the Organization of African Unity, now known as the African Union, and the UN Economic Commission for Africa located their headquarters in Addis Ababa. Ethiopia is also a member of other multilateral African organizations such as the African, Caribbean, and Pacific Group of States and the African Development Bank.

Geopolitical events, most notably the U.S. "war on terror," has strengthened relations among Ethiopia, the United States, and several European nations, despite lingering human rights concerns. Since 2001, Ethiopia has been a key ally in U.S. efforts to curb terrorism in the Horn of Africa region. Tony Blair, the prime minister of Britain, invited his Ethiopian counterpart, Meles Zenawi, to play a leading role on the Commission for Africa, which Blair established to generate new ideas and action for a strong and prosperous Africa. Peacekeeping troops from Ethiopia were sent on UN missions to Korea in the early 1950s, the Congo in the early 1960s, and, more recently, to Burundi, Liberia, and Rwanda.

With the exceptions of Eritrea and Somalia, Ethiopia's relations with the African community are generally constructive and stable. Ethiopia has settled a long-standing border dispute with Sudan and works closely with Djibouti on its land commerce.

THE JUDICIARY

The Ethiopian government has established courts at the state, zonal, district, and local levels in an effort to decentralize the judicial system and relieve the federal judiciary, which is overburdened with a significant backlog of cases.

Although the judicial and legal systems are showing signs of independence, routine abuses of rights by the government occur and severe shortages of personnel and funding hamper effective operation of the courts. The courts in Ethiopia often step in to order the release of government critics jailed on trumped-up charges of treason or armed insurrection. However, judicial action often occurs only after unreasonably long delays, both because of the courts' enormous workload and because of excessive judicial deference to bad-faith police requests for additional time to produce evidence. In addition, courts have shown themselves far less likely to contest prolonged pretrial detention in high-profile cases that have the attention of high-level federal officials.

Fourteen years after the overthrow of the former military government, the Derg, several thousand of its former officials remain jailed awaiting trial, charged with genocide, crimes against humanity, and major felonies. Former dictator Mengistu Haile Mariam, on trial in absentia, remains a guest of the Mugabe government in Zimbabwe, with little chance of being held accountable for his abuses as long as he remains there.

Approximately 2,700 Ethiopian troops serve as peacekeepers in Liberia and Burundi.

ECONOMY

ETHIOPIA IS ONE OF THE WORLD'S poorest countries. With a gross domestic product (GDP) of about $60.3 billion, a per capita annual income of about $900, and chronic trade deficits, it ranks among the bottom 10 on the UN Human Development Index—a composite measure of per capita income, health, and education. Half of the Ethiopian population lives below the poverty line.

Ethiopia's economy has experienced a recent change from being centrally planned to being market oriented. During the Mengistu regime in the mid- to late 1970s, the government exerted state control over the economy, eliminating the preexisting market economy. But after Mengistu was overthrown in 1991, the new transitional government embarked on reforming the economy, including privatizing state enterprises and limiting government regulation. This ongoing process boosted Ethiopia's average GDP growth rate from 2.8 percent during the Derg regime (1974–91) to 4 percent from 1991 to 2003, and 8.9 percent in 2005. The structure of the economy has also changed, with the contribution of agriculture to the GDP falling from 57 percent in 1991 to 40.1 percent in 2005, while that of services rose from 34 percent to 47.2 percent.

The budget has been in deficit since at least the late 1990s, with expenditures regularly exceeding revenues. Shortfalls have been covered by grants and loans from international lending institutions. Ethiopia is heavily dependent on international donor largesse, particularly in times of drought. Since the early 1990s, the country has received financial support for economic reforms from the International Monetary Fund and the World Bank. In 2001 it qualified for debt reduction under these institutions' Heavily Indebted Poor Countries Initiative. On the whole, the reform process has been beneficial; government revenue has risen, and outlays have been redirected from defense to education, health, and

Opposite: **Ethiopian women carry bundles of fodder on their backs. Although most of Ethiopia's workforce is engaged in agriculture, the country is still heavily reliant on foreign food aid due to overpopulation and chronic droughts.**

infrastructure. But, reforms seem to have disproportionately benefited the areas in and around Addis Ababa, and Ethiopia's overall economic performance continues to suffer from hindrances such as public ownership of farmland, low levels of investment, corruption in high levels of the government, and dependence on foreign finance.

AGRICULTURE

Agriculture is by far the most important sector of the Ethiopian economy. In 2005 it constituted half of the country's GDP and 60 percent of exports. About 80 percent of Ethiopians make a living by cultivating crops or raising livestock. The country's transportation and manufacturing sectors rely heavily on agricultural output as well.

Most of Ethiopia's arable land is farmed by peasant families who use only the most basic implements. An example would be the use of oxen for plow agriculture. It is interesting to note that Ethiopia is the only place in Africa where oxen are used in this way. As noted by several economic historians, this is one of the similarities between Ethiopia's feudal system and Europe's. These rural dwellers tend to work on family plots and small-scale farms rather than on commercial farms. As agricultural output

Coffee now accounts for about 60 percent of Ethiopia's export earnings. But when world prices for coffee decline, Ethiopia's second most important export crop, qat, provides a steady income to highland farmers.

OBSTACLES FACING ETHIOPIA'S FARMERS

Unfortunately, neither domestic crop cultivation nor livestock husbandry have been productive enough to feed Ethiopia's growing population adequately. Many believe their country's food supplies are becoming less secure, and reliance on food aid from abroad is still necessary years after the 1984 famine. Several problems continue to hinder agricultural productivity:

- **LACK OF AGRICULTURAL TECHNOLOGY** Few Ethiopian farmers have access to the fertilizers, improved seeds, pesticides, and machinery that are needed to increase crop yields. Instead of tractors and engine-driven plows, for example, most Ethiopians have only hoes, sickles, machetes, and wooden plows to use on their land.
- **POPULATION PRESSURES** Population growth has led to overcrowding, overgrazing, and soil erosion in many drought-prone areas, making farming a difficult and risky undertaking.
- **IRREGULAR RAINFALL** Unpredictable precipitation threatens even those farmers living outside of Ethiopia's most arid regions. Since farming underpins the economy, droughts can cause major humanitarian crises and put the lives of millions of Ethiopians at risk.

remains variable and dependent on the climate, food shortages are still a threat due to irregular rains and inadequate harvests. Until Ethiopia's agricultural sector can be made more productive, reliance on food imports will probably continue.

A number of crops are grown in Ethiopia, but none are as lucrative as the coffee bean. Coffee is the country's main cash crop and greatest foreign exchange earner. A high percentage of Ethiopian coffee is grown in the relatively well-watered southwestern portion of the country. Other products grown by Ethiopian farmers include grains such as teff (indigenous to Ethiopia), wheat, barley, corn, sorghum, and millet. The most common vegetables are chickpeas, lentils, haricot beans, cabbage, onions, and lettuce. Seeds, spices, tobacco, citrus fruit, and bananas are also cultivated.

Ethiopia is estimated to have the largest population of livestock on the African continent. The most common animals herded are sheep, goats, and cattle. Ethiopia is home not only to the largest cattle population in Africa but it is among the top 10 cattle-producing countries in the world. Cattle have proven useful during Ethiopia's periodic droughts and furnish an array of goods for export. In fact, hides, skins, and leather goods are Ethiopia's second-largest exports after coffee.

In 2005 the Ethiopian government, the United Nations, and several international humanitarian organizations appealed for over 600,000 tons (544,200 tonnes) of food relief, valued at around $250 million.

A cotton textile factory at Bahir Dar.

Ethiopia's major imports include machinery and equipment, petroleum, pharmaceuticals, and consumer goods. Its chief trading partners are Germany, Italy, Japan, and the United States.

MANUFACTURING

Manufacturing contributed just over 12 percent of Ethiopia's GDP in 2005. Powered by hydroelectricity, most manufacturing plants are concentrated in Addis Ababa and Dire Dawa and produce consumer goods for the domestic market. Food and beverage processing and textiles dominate the country's manufacturing sector; other manufactured goods include leather goods, sugar and molasses, shoes, tobacco, and beeswax.

The Ethiopian manufacturing sector was plagued by a number of problems in the past, particularly shortages of foreign exchange, new investment, raw materials, and spare parts. The transitional government that took power in 1991 attempted to remedy some of these problems. It loosened investment regulations in an effort to attract foreign capital and offered new tax incentives to potential investors. That 400 new projects were approved in 1992–93 alone testifies to the government's initial success. Today, although the sector is largely supported by foreign assistance inflow, it has experienced a decline in transactions in manufacturing and services, excluding the sectors for infrastructure and finance. Compared with the 22 percent of total transactions in 1988–99, the period from 2000 to 2003 saw a sharp decline of total transactions at a low of 9 percent.

MINING

At present, mining is of only peripheral importance to the Ethiopian economy, contributing less than 1 percent of Ethiopia's GDP. Gold is the only mineral mined on a large scale, with 11,464 pounds (5,200 kg) of it mined in 2001, but the country is known to contain deposits of platinum, salt, limestone, clay, copper, nickel, and iron. Several key mineral discoveries have been announced since the mid-1980s, including iron ore in Welega Province, coal in Kefa, bicarbonate in Shewa, potassium in Tigray, and tantalum near Shakiso. Significant deposits of coal and oil shale were discovered in the western areas of the Illubabor region in December 1994. In order to spark interest in the Ethiopian mining sector, government officials have announced new investment and tax incentive plans, and have visited Western capitals to lobby for investment.

ENERGY

Wood, charcoal, and moving water are the primary sources of energy in Ethiopia. Reliance on wood and charcoal for energy and construction needs has contributed to the deforestation of much of the highlands during the last three decades. Hydropower meets about 90 percent of the country's electricity needs but this also means that electricity generation, like agriculture, is dependent on rainfall, which is unreliable in Ethiopia. Fortunately, natural gas reserves have been discovered and plans are afoot to exploit the estimated 440 trillion cubic feet (12.5 trillion cubic m) of gas in the southeastern lowlands region. Exploration for oil is under way in the Gambela region bordering Sudan. However, Ethiopia still has to import a large share of its petroleum to support the country's energy and construction needs.

TRANSPORTATION

Ethiopia's transportation system is inadequate by any standard, needing both upgrades and expansion. The country has about 23,002 miles (37,018 km) of roadways, of which only 39 percent are in good condition, according to the Ethiopian Roads Authority. Many of the country's paved

Less than half of Ethiopia's towns and cities are connected to the national electrical grid.

Although Ethiopia's rivers are generally not navigable, cargo-carrying boats do ply the waters of Lake Tana and a few Rift Valley lakes. Boats constructed of reeds for travel on Lake Tana are known as *tankwas* (TAHN-kwahs).

roads are in poor condition due to the damage they sustained during the secessionist wars of the 1980s. In addition, Ethiopia's mountainous terrain has made reaching remote areas notoriously difficult. Ethiopian officials are committed to repairing the damage to the country's roads, and have allocated about 75 percent of the government's transportation budget to improving the road network. In 1998 the World Bank approved a $309 million loan to help fund efforts to improve roads in Ethiopia. In 2003 work began on the second phase of the Road Sector Development Program, scheduled to upgrade 80 percent of paved and 63 percent of unpaved roads by 2007.

The only working railroad in Ethiopia is the Addis to Djibouti line. Its poor condition has caused several serious accidents since the mid-1980s. Some repairs have been carried out, but much more work needs to be done to make the line safe and reliable. In an effort to reduce dependence on Djibouti, Ethiopia announced in 2001 that it had reached an agreement with Sudan to build a rail link to Port Sudan. At a cost of $1.5 billion, the project is not likely to be started any time soon.

Ethiopia is served by international airports at Addis Ababa, Dire Dawa, and several regional airports. Ethiopian Airlines, which delivers reliable and efficient service to domestic and international destinations, has been called one of Africa's success stories. Started in 1946, it is one of Africa's oldest airlines, and is proud to have mainly Ethiopians making up its pilot crew. Ethiopian Airlines offers flights to many African capitals, and carries more cargo than any other airline on the continent.

ENCOURAGING TOURISM

The EPRDF government has revived the Ethiopian tourist industry, after its dramatic slump during the Mengistu era. Besides making it easier for prospective tourists to qualify for visas and travel out of the capital, a number of new hotels are under construction in the capital and other popular tourist centers. A major three-phase renovation and expansion of Bole International Airport in Addis Ababa was announced in 2001. When completed, the airport will be handling an estimated 6 to 7 million passengers annually, a twelve-fold jump from its current capacity of 500,000 passengers. In 2004 the Ethiopian Tourism Commission claimed that nearly 210,000 tourists visited Ethiopia, spending $100 million in total. Most of the visitors came for the country's natural and historical attractions; others were there to attend international conferences and meetings and to conduct business.

Ethiopia has no shortage of attractions for the adventurous tourist. Addis Ababa is rich with cultural diversity and contains many places of interest. The countryside beyond the capital is home to fascinating ancient ruins such as the castles of Gondar (*one of which is shown above*), the rock-hewn churches of Lalibela, and the obelisks at Axum. Scenic wonders also abound. Not to be missed are the Blue Nile Gorge and the Blue Nile Falls near the town of Bahir Dar on Lake Tana. The Great Rift Valley lakes region is home to beaches, wildlife, and a popular hot springs resort. The Simien Mountains in the northwestern part of the country are renowned for their wildlife and scenic beauty. Wherever they choose to visit, most travelers soon discover why Ethiopia is known as "the Land of 13 Months of Sunshine."

ENVIRONMENT

A LAND OF RUGGED MOUNTAINS, expansive savannas, lakes, and rivers, Ethiopia has long been recognized for its wealth of natural resources, endemic wildlife species, and biodiversity. The Great Rift Valley is a unique region of volcanic lakes, steep ridges, and spectacular vistas. The Blue Nile Falls is one of Africa's greatest natural wonders.

With 14 national parks and wildlife reserves, Ethiopia has preserved a microcosm of the entire sub-Saharan ecosystem. Birdlife abounds and indigenous animals, from monkeys to the rare Walia ibex, roam free. After the rains, the country is decked with flowers and is home to more native plants than most countries in Africa. Ethiopia's natural beauty has amazed visitors, but the country's environmental concerns are significant and are threatening the livelihood and well-being of its citizens, who are actually the key culprits of the environmental degradation.

ENVIRONMENTAL CONCERNS

The key environmental concern Ethiopia faces today is overpopulation, which results in overgrazing, overcultivation, soil erosion, deforestation, and desertification. Forest fires are also of critical concern.

More than 80 percent of Ethiopians, or about 70 million people, live in the country's highlands, where human and livestock population densities are very high and the overwhelming majority of Ethiopians earn their livelihoods from agricultural activities. The struggle to survive has resulted in a myriad of severe environmental concerns. Overgrazing and overcultivation have resulted in massive soil erosion, which affects 82 percent of the country. About 1 billion tons (907 billion kg) of topsoil is eroded annually, depleting the fertility of the land. There has also been a loss of vegetation cover and biodiversity due to deforestation

Opposite: **The Blue Nile Falls, called Tis Issat in Amharic, is fed by the waters of Lake Tana. It is the second largest waterfall in Africa.**

and desertification. In 1900 approximately 30 percent of Ethiopia was covered by forest but, by the mid-1980s this figure had fallen to less than 30 percent as forests were cleared to make room for agricultural cultivation. The gradual spread of the desert has shrunk the amount of land suitable for agriculture. From 1992 to 2002 there were 6,603 species of known plants, 277 species of mammals, and 262 bird species in the country. Since then 22 plant species along with 35 mammal and 22 bird species have become threatened.

Environmental degradation has had severe socioeconomic consequences for Ethiopians. With soil erosion, the depletion of soil fertility, desertification, and decreasing biodiversity, access to a variety of food and income sources has become increasingly difficult. Per capita food production has declined since the 1970s and food shortages are endemic in the Ethiopian highlands, where desertification is particularly severe and rainfall is marginal or unreliable. According to the United Nations and the World Bank, Ethiopia currently suffers from a food deficit so severe that even in the most productive year, at least 5 million Ethiopians require food aid. The United Nations and the World Bank maintain that without immediate steps to deal with the burgeoning population, large-scale environmental degradation, soil exhaustion, and rural land-holding policies, Ethiopia will become permanently reliant upon donor largesse just to feed itself.

PROTECTED AREAS

Ethiopia is home to 14 national parks and wildlife sanctuaries. These key biodiversity areas harbor the finest and most intact remnants of the highlands' original vegetation. They are also home to four threatened endemic species and to more than half of the global population of the Ethiopian wolf. What is even more remarkable is that more than 30 of the 200

mammal species found in the Ethiopian highlands are found nowhere else, including three rodents and one primate—the gelada.

However, sharing these environmentally precious highlands are 70 million Ethiopians and their thousands of livestock. According to Conservation International, Ethiopia has the largest herd of domestic livestock and cattle in Africa. In protected areas like the Senkele Sanctuary, Netchsar National Park, Mago National Park, Awash National Park, and Simien Mountains National Park, thousands of cattle, goats, and sheep overrun the parks. These livestock increasingly must use areas with poor soil fertility to graze, and overgrazing has led to soil erosion and heightened competition between livestock and wildlife.

Complicating this mix are the intensive agricultural cultivation and human settlements in the area. Given the rapid conversion of natural habitats to areas of cultivation needed to feed the ever-increasing population, it is not surprising that almost all wildlife-sustaining habitats are being destroyed. In the Bale Mountains are an estimated 300 (of the global total estimate of 500) Ethiopian wolves. In 2003 an outbreak of rabies killed

Gelada baboons in Simien Mountains National Park. These primates can only be found in Ethiopia. Like the other wild animals in Ethiopia, the gelada is being threatened by the loss of natural habitats resulting from human activities.

A breathtaking vista of the flora and natural landscape in the Bale Mountains National Park.

20 wolves in the Web valley within the Bale area. It is believed that the disease was carried by immigrant domestic dogs accompanying people and livestock in their seasonal search for grazing.

Hunting is also a significant problem in the Ethiopian highlands. Almost all the wildlife has been killed for food by tribal peoples, such as the Ari, Bana, Mursi, and Karo. Very few numbers of Beisa oryx, Grant's gazelle, and topi, formerly in the thousands, remain at all.

As the national parks are not adequately secured, staffed, or equipped, human causes of wildlife devastation cannot be stopped. These difficulties have been exacerbated by famines, refugee problems, civil unrest, armed rebellions, and war, which threaten the livelihood of people and make it unlikely that conservation measures will be enforced.

Currently, a few isolated pockets remain in Ethiopia where the depletion of vulnerable or endangered wildlife species is still considered reversible (i.e., the Bale, Arusi and Simien mountains and the Denakil Desert). Outside recognized conservation areas, several remote locations of relatively low human population and activity, with quite high densities of wildlife, have been identified for sustainable use.

ETHIOPIA'S KEY NATIONAL PARKS

SIMIEN MOUNTAINS NATIONAL PARK Home of the Ras Deshen Peak, the fourth-highest mountain in Africa, the Simien Mountain National Park was created primarily to protect the 1,000 or so Walia ibex that are said to live in the park. Also found in the park are families of the unique gelada baboon, with its scarlet bleeding heart on its chest, and the rare Simien fox. The Simien fox, although named after the mountains, is rarely seen by the visitor. It is more likely to be seen in the Bale National Park. Over 50 species of birds have been sighted in the Simien Mountains.

AWASH NATIONAL PARK Lying in the lowlands to the east of Addis Ababa, the Awash National Park is one of the finest reserves in Ethiopia. Awash National Park, surrounding the dormant volcano of Fantale, is a reserve of arid and semiarid woodland and savanna, with forests along the Awash River. Forty-six species of animals have been identified here, including beisa oryx and Swayne's hartebeest. The birdlife is prolific, especially along the river and on the nearby Lake Basaka, and there are endemic ones among the 392 species recorded.

OMO NATIONAL PARK One of the most beautiful national parks in Ethiopia, the Omo National Park is home to an amazing range of wildlife. About 306 species of birds have been identified here, while large herds of eland, some buffalo, elephants, giraffes, cheetahs, lions, leopards, and Burchell's zebras are not uncommon.

MAGO NATIONAL PARK Covering an area of 1,343 miles (2,162 km) on the banks of the Omo River, the Mago National Park is relatively undeveloped for tourists. The broad grasslands teem with herds of buffalo, giraffe, elephants, and kudu, while sometimes it is possible to find lions, leopards, and Burchell's zebras. The abundant birdlife here is typical of dry grasslands and riverbanks.

GAMBALA NATIONAL PARK Many interesting species of animals and birds can often be seen here. According to the Wildlife Information Office, Dowsett Forbs has identified hundreds of species of birds—596 residents and 224 regular seasonal migrants residing in the park.

BALE MOUNTAINS NATIONAL PARK The Bale Mountains include Ethiopia's second-highest mountain but are not as rugged as the Simiens. The region is home to several of Ethiopia's endemic animals, including the Simien fox and mountain nyala.

CONSERVATION EFFORTS

While Ethiopia is blessed with abundant natural assets, these endowments remained largely unprotected until the mid-1960s, when the government instituted a conservation and protected areas program. This resulted in bylaws and areas for conservation and protection of a variety of species and habitats. Since then, Ethiopia has enacted a wide range of laws aimed at protecting the environment. The incorporation of environmental rights under the constitution, the adoption of the Environmental Policy and the Conservation Strategy of Ethiopia, the ratification of multilateral environmental conventions, and the establishment of the Environmental Protection Authority are some of the basic steps taken toward environmental protection and sustainable development.

The results, however, have not been spectacular. According to the International Union for Conservation of Nature and Natural Resources (IUCN), as of 2003 only 7.5 million acres (3 million ha) of land in the country has been classified as protected areas under the category of nature reserves, wilderness areas, and national parks, while 32.3 million acres (13.1 million ha) has been unclassified or categorized as areas managed for sustainable use. Moreover, all the conservation efforts have not been able to stop people from threatening the wildlife and vegetation within the protected areas. The inadequacy of Ethiopia's conservation efforts can be attributed to several factors, including ineffective deterrents, such as fines that are modest compared with the gains that would be gotten from noncompliance, and the lack of specific regulations and laws, standards, and guidelines that could be implemented and monitored.

Ironically, the era of Mengistu, who carried out the Red Terror purges that led to thousands of humans being killed, was a time of peaceful increase for most of the wildlife populations in Ethiopia. Under the Derg,

A male mountain nyala in Bale National Park.

the government played an active role in forest management, using harsh enforcement practices to ensure that the forests were preserved. As a result, people refrained from environment-damaging activities and the forests were well preserved. Correspondingly, the numbers of wildlife in the protected areas increased dramatically. For instance, mountain nyalas in the Dinsho area, the Gaysay Valley, and Gaysay Mountains increased from about 1,000 to over 3,000 during this period.

However, within one week of the fall of Mengistu's military regime and following the announcement by the new prime minister, Meles Zenawi, that all the land in Ethiopia belonged to the people, the areas of the parks were resettled by farmers and nomads, and they continued to expand their land settlements, year by year, until all semblance of the designated National Parks' boundaries have been erased.

ETHIOPIANS

ONE OF THE MOST REMARKABLE aspects of Ethiopia is its cultural diversity. The country is home to more than 100 different ethnic groups, the largest of which are the Oromo, Amhara, Tigray, and Somali. More than 70 different languages are spoken in the country. Ethiopia's diversity has greatly enriched the country over the centuries, but it has also led to conflict.

The Amhara group played a dominant role through much of Ethiopia's history, but resistance to Amhara power became widespread in the late 1970s. Undeterred by Mengistu's military might, ethnic secessionist movements led by Eritreans, Oromos, Tigrayans, and Somalis severely threatened Ethiopian unity. By 1991, the Eritreans had won their independence, and the EPRDF—made up mostly of Tigrayans—toppled the Mengistu government.

Boundaries between ethnic groups are not necessarily static. In Ethiopia—as in some other African countries—the character of ethnic groups can change as people mix with others of different backgrounds through trade, intermarriage, and friendship.

Left: **A Somali family.**

Opposite: **A Hamar woman from southern Ethiopia. The Hamar are a minority ethnic group who mainly raise livestock.**

POPULATION

In 2006 approximately 74.8 million people lived in Ethiopia, 85 percent of whom lived in rural areas, cultivating crops, or herding livestock. The country's birthrate in 2006 was 37.98 births per 1,000 people, a high figure compared with the rest of the developing world. It's death rate of 14.86 deaths per 1,000 people is more typical of developing nations. Ethiopia's infant mortality rate in 2005 was approximately 94 per 1,000 live births. The reasons for the high infant mortality rate include Ethiopia's lack of health care facilities, the spread of infectious diseases, poor sanitation, malnutrition, and food shortages. These factors, combined with the AIDS epidemic, make the life expectancy of Ethiopians one of the lowest in the world. Current figures estimate that Ethiopian

Children under 15 made up almost 44 percent of Ethiopia's population in 2004, a consequence of the country's high birthrate.

women can expect to live for approximately 50 years and Ethiopian men for approximately 48 years.

ETHNIC GROUPS

The Oromo people constitute 40 percent of Ethiopia's population and are the country's largest ethnic group. Ancestors of contemporary Oromo society started to spread out from their original homeland in the south central highlands in the 16th century. Today their descendants live in central, southern, and western Ethiopia. Although the members of this ethnic group come from a line of pastoralists and nomads and share the Oromo language, there is much diversity within the group. For example, some Oromo live in decentralized groups, while others live in communities characterized by hierarchical authority structures. Religious beliefs among the Oromo can vary as well. Some Oromo hold traditional beliefs, while other family members may practice Islam or Orthodox Christianity.

The Amhara and Tigray combined make up 32 percent of Ethiopia's population. The dominant group during centuries of imperial rule, the Amhara have continued to play a leading role in Ethiopian politics, despite their minority status. The Amhara language, Amharic, has long been

Amharic is the official language of Ethiopia and the native tongue of the Amhara ethnic group.

A Tigray man. The Tigray number no more than 10 percent of Ethiopia's population.

the favored medium of communication in government, commerce, and education, and is the official language of Ethiopia. Most of the Amhara belong to the Ethiopian Orthodox Church and tend farms in the Ethiopian highlands, where they cultivate teff, barley, wheat, sorghum, corn, and peas, and herd cattle, sheep, and goats. Occasional conflicts among the Amhara of different regions attest to the group's lack of cohesiveness.

Like the Amhara, the Tigray also farm in the highlands and tend to belong to the Ethiopian Orthodox Church. The Tigray are known for having founded the kingdom of Axum in the early centuries of the Christian era. Their descendants have lived in the area around Axum for centuries, and because of this, the soil in the region has become largely exhausted. The resulting poor harvests have led many Tigray to move to other areas of the country in search of better land. The Tigray speak Tigrinya, a Semitic language related to Amharic.

The fourth key ethnic group is the Sidama. They constitute 9 percent of the total Ethiopian population. The Sidama people occupy a densely populated area in southwestern Ethiopia that is reputed for its fertile soil. An agricultural people, they grow grain crops, coffee, tobacco, and a banana-like crop known as *enset*. They also raise cattle, sheep, and horses. Like other Ethiopians, religious observance among the Sidama can involve traditional beliefs, Christianity, or Islam.

OTHER GROUPS IN ETHIOPIA

SOMALIS Predominantly pastoralists, the Somalis are concentrated in the Ogaden, the region in the southeastern lowlands near the border with Somalia. Many Somalis are Muslims whose ancestors converted to Islam around the 12th century.

SHANKELLA The Shankella, an ethnic group that constitutes approximately 6 percent of the population, occupies the western part of the country from the border of Eritrea to Lake Turkana.

AFAR Sometimes referred to as the Danakil, the Afar people live in the rocky, arid countryside between the highlands and the Red Sea. The Afar people are mainly pastoralists.

GURAGE The Gurage reside in the southern Shewa region, just north of their Sidama neighbors. They are also agriculturalists whose religious beliefs can vary. However, unlike the Sidama, the Gurage have established a notable presence in Ethiopia's urban areas, where they engage in trade, manual labor, and other service occupations.

PEOPLES ALONG THE ETHIOPIA-SUDAN BORDER These groups include the Nara, Kunama, Gumuz, Berta, Anuak, and Nuer. They occupy remote lowland areas near Sudan and speak Nilo-Saharan languages, unlike the rest of Ethiopians (the majority of Ethiopians speak Afro-Asiatic languages). Many of these borderland peoples are descendants of slaves held by Ethiopian and Sudanese Arabs in the 19th and early 20th centuries. Today these groups engage in cultivation, herding, and fishing. Their remote location has long kept them on the periphery of Ethiopian society. *(Shown above are two Bena women from southwestern Ethiopia.)*

SOCIAL STRATIFICATION

During the era of imperial rule, social status in Ethiopia depended on the amount of land one owned. But once the old order was overthrown and Mengistu came to power, land was nationalized, so social status became more closely tied to one's political influence. Party members, government ministers, military officers, and senior civil servants became the new elite from the mid-1970s onward.

Today Ethiopians tend to view government work, military service, religious leadership, and farming as the most desirable occupations. Forming the middle class in Ethiopia are those in the bureaucracy and the professionals, many of whom have gained advanced educational training. Middle-class Ethiopians are highly urbanized and frequently marry across ethnic boundaries. Many in this class left the country during the Mengistu

During the long era of imperial rule, most government officials and landowners in Ethiopia were Amhara.

The manager of a textile factory in Bahir Dar.

STYLES OF DRESS AND ADORNMENT

One of the most distinctive articles of clothing for rural Ethiopians is the *shamma* (SHEH-mah), a one-piece cotton wrap worn over the shoulders and arms. (*on the right two women are shown wearing the* shamma).Worn by both men and women, the *shamma* is particularly common among the Amhara and Tigray peoples. This garment often features a colorful border and is sometimes worn for ceremonial occasions by city dwellers as well as country people. In the higher mountainous regions the *shamma* is useful in keeping out the cold wind.

Another traditional costume is the *k'amis* (kah-MEES), a white cotton gown that women sometimes wear beneath the *shamma*. Western-style dress is now a common sight in urban areas, although people may wear more traditional clothing at home.

Earrings, bracelets, necklaces, and religious emblems are popular forms of adornment in Ethiopia and are often made of beads or shells. Oromo women are known for their attractive necklaces, while Tigray women are famous for their gold jewelry. Scarves and turbans are worn by women throughout the country. Men in the rural areas often carry walking sticks—known in Ethiopia as *dulas* (DOO-luhs)—as they roam the countryside.

era due to a mixture of fear and disenchantment. People engaged in commerce and trade—many of whom are Muslims or non-Ethiopians—have yet to enjoy the respect that is bestowed upon bureaucrats and professionals.

LIFESTYLE

JUST AS THERE IS NO single Ethiopian culture, there is no single Ethiopian lifestyle. The country's cultural diversity has created many different lifestyles that vary according to religion, ethnicity, gender, generation, and locale (rural versus urban, highlands versus lowlands).

An observation that is often made about Ethiopian society is that the family is all-important. It is the

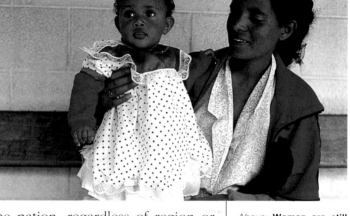

Above: **Women are still primarily responsible for child care in most Ethiopian families. Ethiopia is traditionally a highly patriarchal society.**

Opposite: **A classroom in a Christian missionary school. Primary-level education is compulsory in Ethiopia.**

basic social and economic unit of the nation, regardless of region or ethnic group. Ethiopian families tend to be larger than North American families—the average size of an Ethiopian household is 4.8 people compared with North America's 2.6 people. This is partly because parents fear that some of their offspring will die from famine or disease. Sometimes families are nuclear, consisting only of parents and their children. Other Ethiopian families are extended, meaning that an assortment of aunts, uncles, cousins, and grandparents share the household.

Families in Ethiopia tend to be patriarchal rather than matriarchal, but women are crucial in holding families together. The division of labor between men and women is usually well defined, especially in rural areas. Men are expected to plant, weed, and harvest the family's crops; women, besides helping with the farmwork, cook and prepare food, maintain the home, and assume primary responsibility for child care. Although family roles are changing in some areas, elders are still treated with great respect.

NAMING CHILDREN IN ETHIOPIA

Often Ethiopian children are not given names until they are several weeks old, when their character begins to show itself. Before then, parents may just use informal terms of endearment to refer to their infants. Highland societies tend to invest children's names with meaning to reflect parents' wishes or hopes. Here are some examples:

NAME	MEANING	NAME	MEANING
Addis	The new one	Negga	It dawned.
Ageritu	The little country	Nur Addis	New life
Allefnew	We made it through the bad times.	Sintayyehu	I have seen so much.
Attalel	May he or she trick death.	Tesfaye	My hope
Bayyush	If only they had seen you.	Tsehay	The sun
Biyadgillign	If only he would grow up for me.	Zemach	The campaigner
Hull Agerish	Your land is everywhere.		

Some traditional societies in Ethiopia view having twins as a sign of bad luck.

BIRTH AND CHILDHOOD

Like many developing countries, Ethiopia has a high infant mortality rate, and this explains why births are sometimes greeted cautiously by parents, especially fathers. Only a minority of Ethiopian children are born in hospitals. Most are born in rural households, where elderly women often serve as midwives to assist expectant mothers. In families belonging to the Ethiopian Orthodox Church, boys are baptized on the 40th day after birth and girls on the 80th. Sometimes children are given a special baptismal name that remains a secret or is used only by the immediate family. Friends and relatives are usually invited to baptism ceremonies, and they help mark the occasion by serving food and drink.

Ethiopian children are given responsibilities at an early age. When they reach just about 5 years of age, rural children may be asked to help

gather firewood or feed their family's chickens. When they are a little older, children often help guard their family's fields from intruders such as birds or baboons. Boys are eventually expected to help herd goats and cattle, while girls generally help grind grain, prepare meals, and care for younger children.

Childhood in rural Ethiopia is not all work, however. Children have ample time for play and often participate in games and recreational activities with their peers. Young people also participate fully in religious festivals, during which they can enjoy feasts, dances, music, and fellowship.

Circumcision traditionally marks the transition from childhood to adulthood for boys and girls in traditional African societies, but in Ethiopia, some children are circumcised a few weeks after birth. Sometimes, circumcision occurs when children are older; in Oromo society, for example, girls are not circumcised until just before marriage. Female circumcision consists of cutting the clitoral hood and in some cases, the entire clitoris. This practice, although considered offensive and cruel by Western societies, is deeply cultural and is seen as an effective way to ensure the sexual purity of girls.

A bride and groom lead a wedding procession. Cattle are often given as bridewealth in rural Ethiopia. In some groups, the groom is also expected to give the bride a special dress as a wedding gift, often accompanied by a waistband, shawl, scarf, or shoes.

MARRIAGE

Although marital practices in Ethiopia vary according to ethnic group, some generalizations can be made. Women often marry while still in their teens, while men tend to marry in their late teens or early 20s. Marriages can occur across religious lines—between Christians and Muslims, for example—but in these cases, either the bride or the groom usually converts. Marriages rarely cross both religious and ethnic lines.

Negotiations between the bride's family and the groom's family typically take place prior to the wedding and involve both male and female elders. The groom's family is usually expected to offer a gift to the bride's family, to compensate them for their loss. This gift, known as bridewealth, is given in many traditional African societies to sanction marriage. In most cases, if a marriage ends in divorce, the bridewealth is returned to the groom's family.

Marriage

Ethiopian weddings tend to involve an elaborate array of rituals. Some groups hold solemn engagement ceremonies prior to weddings. In one such ceremony, the groom's mother anoints her son and his best man on the forehead and knee, then leads a procession to the bride's family home. There, the groom and the best man are anointed by the bride's mother. In some Muslim wedding ceremonies, the groom and the best man have black markings drawn around their eyes and crosses painted on their foreheads. They then join a wedding procession led by elders carrying fly whisks and wearing fine clothes. Ethiopian wedding ceremonies are usually presided over by a religious official who witnesses the exchange of vows between the bride and groom.

Weddings are cause for celebration, and those in Ethiopia are no exception. Dances and chanting competitions are sometimes held after wedding ceremonies, and feasts commonly accompany weddings. In many wedding receptions, the groomsmen will share the same table, while the bride and groom exchange mouthfuls of food in front of the assembled guests. Following the celebrations, many newlyweds go on a honeymoon in which they stay in a special hut and enjoy attentive service from the groomsmen. Such honeymoons typically last one or two weeks.

A wedding ceremony in Axum.

A Christian funeral procession.

DEATH

The customs surrounding death in Ethiopia also differ according to religion, ethnicity, and region. In most highland societies, funerals can take several days and draw even more people than weddings. Two terms are commonly used in the highlands to refer to funeral ceremonies: *merdo* (MUHR-doh), which means announcement of death, and *legso* (LEHK-soh), which refers to mourning. Christian communities often have restrictions governing proper burials. For example, such communities may refuse to give a Christian burial to a suicide victim or a person who married a Muslim. They also often oppose burying Christians in the same cemeteries with Muslims.

Burial associations are common among Ethiopians. Besides providing members with a sense of community, these associations ensure that their members will be given a proper burial. Members are expected to attend the funerals of association members and to make regular contributions to the association. Typical contributions include wood, water, grain, money, and prepared food items. Most burial associations have a leader or leaders who collect donations and enforce rules. In rural Wello society, such associations are known as the *qire* (KEE-ray); in some Amhara areas, the term used is *iddir* (ID-ir).

Dying Amharas receive absolution from a priest, who also presides over the burial. A priest then leads a memorial celebration 40 days after the death.

SURMA FUNERAL RITUALS

The Surma people live in extreme southwestern Ethiopia, near the Kenyan and Sudanese borders. In the late 1980s, two photojournalists, Carol Beckwith and Angela Fisher, documented Surma cultural life in a series of vivid photographs that were eventually published in *National Geographic* and the book *African Ark*. In the course of their work, Beckwith and Fisher learned a great deal about Surma funeral rituals and captured some of these rituals on film.

In one Surma funeral observed by the photographers, the deceased person's body was wrapped in hides in preparation for burial. After milk was poured into the deceased's ears, the body was positioned in a vertical, sitting position in the grave. Participants in the funeral placed some of the deceased's possessions in the grave alongside the body. As in many Surma funerals, an elder told the story of the deceased's life through a series of chants. After that was done, others in the ceremony sounded horns made of animal tusks.

Many rural dwellers live in one-room houses made of wood, straw, and clay, with wooden, grass, or tin roofs. Furniture is usually limited to a table, stools, and beds made of wood or animal skins.

RURAL LIVING

Approximately 90 percent of Ethiopians make their living from the land. After the imperial government was toppled in 1974, private land ownership was abolished. The nobles and landowners who had controlled so much of the land were forced to surrender their privileges to the new regime. The land redistribution program mandated by the Mengistu-led government involved forcing thousands of peasants onto collective farms. Private property rights were reinstated by the new transitional government in the early 1990s, and the mandatory collective farming programs have been discontinued.

Housing styles in the Ethiopian countryside vary by region and ethnic group. Cooking is done in a fireplace in the middle of the house. Sometimes, families reserve a corner of their home for a few of their domesticated animals. Although villages can be found throughout Ethiopia, more common are smaller clusters of two to four homes surrounded by fields and gardens.

Nomadic Ethiopians—most of whom live in the arid lowland regions— often live in portable homes constructed of branches, grass, and animal skins. These homes are easily disassembled and transported on the backs of camels as the nomads travel the plains looking for new grasslands and sources of water. Northern rural dwellers sometimes live in houses made of stone.

URBAN LIVING

Housing in Ethiopia's cities reflects patterns of social inequality and thus varies a great deal. Some high government officials and prosperous business people live in spacious homes with appliances, telephones, and several cars. Members of the urban underclass, on the other hand, are sometimes forced by economic circumstance to live in small tin shacks without running water or electricity. Urban poverty is a serious problem in Addis Ababa, giving rise to overcrowding, homelessness, and an increasing number of street children. Inadequate municipal governance in providing sanitary living conditions and access to clean water and electricity exacerbates urban poverty and makes the cities hotbeds for crime and diseases.

Although living in Addis Ababa brings with it many opportunities, shortages of kerosene, sugar, and salt have made life hard in recent years.

Urbanization has altered traditional family structures and social roles in Ethiopia. Whereas rural women tend to be confined to household tasks, women in urban areas have more opportunities to work outside the home, for example, in schools, businesses, hotels, and restaurants. The urban environment has also affected young people's lives. As the demand for housing and well-paying jobs in Addis Ababa often exceeds the supply, many young adults have felt obligated to postpone marriage until they achieve economic security and independence. This often takes longer in the city than it does in the countryside.

ETHIOPIAN WOMEN

Women have traditionally been relegated to a subordinate status in Ethiopian society. They have faced persistent discrimination and have had fewer opportunities for education and employment outside of the home. However, as Ethiopia has changed, so too has the role of women.

In the rural areas women are expected to be wives and mothers first and foremost. Women's tasks typically include raising children, maintaining the household, grinding corn, carrying loads, washing clothing, and helping with the farmwork. Hard physical labor is something that most rural women are used to. Cooking in particular takes up a large chunk of their time. But women's roles began to change somewhat in the 1970s and 1980s, as Ethiopia's wars took many men away from their homesteads. Women were left to do the bulk of the farming, support the family, and care for the children and older relatives on their own. Many women thus became the heads of their households and emerged from this era with new responsibilities and a heightened sense of independence.

Although women have traditionally been confined to homemaking, there has been a rise in the number of working women in the past few decades. According to a survey in 2000, 57 percent of Ethiopian women were gainfully employed.

Urban Ethiopian women usually have more opportunities for education, health care, and employment than their rural counterparts. Women in cities and towns have typically worked in the service sector, in establishments such as hotels and restaurants. Other employment opportunities for urban women include factory work and sales. A survey undertaken in Addis Ababa in the mid-1970s demonstrated that female factory workers earned only about 25 percent of the wages paid to men for the same work. Even though the constitution states that all persons are equal before the law and that there shall be no discrimination based on gender, age, religion, and so forth, there have been no effective enforcements of this law. But, despite this history of discrimination, many women regard cities as places where economic independence can be achieved. Some flee the rural areas in order to escape arranged or unhappy marriages; they quickly find work in Addis Ababa as waitresses or domestic servants. Some women even travel as far as the Middle East to seek employment as industrial or domestic workers, with Lebanon being the most popular destination.

SCHOOLS AND STUDENTS

Improving educational opportunities for a large and dispersed population has been one of modern Ethiopia's major challenges. In 1974 the literacy rate in Ethiopia was less than 10 percent. The Mengistu regime undertook a massive literacy campaign beginning in the late 1970s and claimed that the country's literacy rate had increased to 63 percent by 1984. Although this was probably an inflated figure, strides were undoubtedly made. In 2003 UNESCO estimated that the literacy rate among Ethiopians was 42.7 percent.

In 2001, 47 percent of children in the relevant age group were enrolled in primary schools. Attendance among girls, at 41 percent, lagged behind

Although the Mengistu government was not known for appointing large numbers of women to high office, it did improve educational opportunities for women. During the 1970s and 1980s the literacy rate for women increased significantly.

ETHIOPIANS ABROAD

Between 1974 and 1991 approximately 3.5 million Ethiopians left their country in search of a better life. Another 20,000 people fled immediately after the fall of the Mengistu regime in mid-1991. Many of those who fled during the Mengistu era did so to escape violence and political persecution; others left because of religious or ethnic discrimination. Some emigrants left in search of better economic opportunities.

Neighboring countries in East Africa and the Horn absorbed many of the Ethiopians. In the mid-1980s thousands of Ethiopians fled into Sudan, Djibouti, and Somalia to escape warfare. By 1988 over half a million Ethiopian refugees were living in Sudan alone. This mass exodus of Ethiopians resulted in a serious humanitarian crisis, as the refugees' need for food, shelter, and medical supplies far outstripped Sudan's ability to provide.

Many Ethiopians settled in the United States during this same period. Although some sought U.S. citizenship, many still actively monitored the political situation back home, sometimes staging meetings and marches or publishing newsletters relating to current events in Ethiopia. The struggle for Ethiopians living in the United States has been to adjust to a new culture without losing touch with their Ethiopian heritage. Sizable communities of Ethiopian expatriates now exist in metropolitan areas such as Washington, D.C. and the San Francisco Bay Area.

Besides regular schools, Ethiopia has technical, adult, and night schools and an array of teacher training programs. A college for the training of civil servants opened in Addis Ababa in 1994.

that among boys, at 53 percent. For secondary schools, enrollment was 13 percent (15 percent of boys and 10 percent of girls). Urban schools tend to be more numerous and better equipped than rural ones, which are often relatively inaccessible due to the country's underdeveloped transportation network. Rural schools have long suffered from poor facilities and shortages of teaching staff. Since many rural families are traditionally reluctant to send their daughters to school, students in the countryside are predominantly male. Girls growing up in the cities, however, are more likely to attend school than their rural counterparts, and they can now attend a university if they score well enough in national examinations.

Education is free from primary through university level. Primary education from grades one to six begins at 7 years of age. Secondary education from grades seven to twelve begins at 13 years of age. Education is compulsory at the primary level and primary schools are scattered across the countryside. Thereafter, access to facilities determines further education, which may explain why children attending secondary schools are more prevalent in larger urban areas. Consequently, enrollments decline drastically from

Two Ethiopian boys read aloud. Children start primary school at 7 years of age. Education in Ethiopia is free at primary level.

the primary to the secondary level, and secondary school facilities are severely overtaxed.

Ethiopia has approximately a dozen universities and colleges providing technical, teaching, and other professional training, but the country's most prestigious institution of higher learning is Addis Ababa University. Established in 1950 as Haile Selassie I University, the institution was renamed by the Socialist government in the mid-1970s. As it stands now, higher education is still beyond the reach of most Ethiopians. The exceptions are in Addis Ababa. In recent years, a number of private schools have sprung up to meet the demand for university-level instruction in the capital city, as space limitations at Addis Ababa University make for an extremely competitive admissions process at the premier institution.

The educational system in Ethiopia clearly faces many challenges. Due to rural economic conditions, many families have trouble finding money for their children's school supplies. They also find it difficult to send their children to school when they are needed to herd livestock, work in the fields, and help with domestic chores. These socioeconomic realities have made finishing high school difficult for most rural youths. Wartime damage to schools and shortages of teachers, books, and desks only add to these problems. But with the right combination of internal

At the World Education Forum in 2000 the Ethiopian government committed itself to universalizing primary education in the country by 2015.

73

A man cradles his friend, who is stricken with malaria. Like HIV/AIDS, this mosquito-borne disease is one of the leading causes of death in Ethiopia.

political stability, economic development, and international assistance, education in Ethiopia will continue to improve.

LIVING WITH AIDS

The acquired immune defiency syndrome (AIDS) epidemic has reached alarming proportions in Ethiopia. At the end of 2003 the UN reported that 4.4 percent of the population, or about 1.5 million Ethiopian adults, was suffering from AIDS or human immunodeficiency virus (HIV), the forerunner of AIDS. Compared with the 1.8 million infected with HIV/AIDS in the whole of Latin America and the 1.6 million in Eastern Europe and Central Asia, the number of infected Ethiopians is indeed high. The average life expectancy of an Ethiopian is currently 49 years. The U.S. Census Bureau has projected that the life expectancy in Ethiopia will decline to about 42 years by 2010 because of AIDS.

HIV is generally spread through sexual contact, intravenous drug use, or perinatal transmission, which means the disease is spread from mother to newborn. Many of the infected, for fear of being ostracized, refrain from revealing their health status, thus enabling the infection to spread further. In addition, poverty makes medical treatment inaccessible. Having a significant number of the population affected by AIDS is economically draining. The vicious cycle of poverty is made even more pronounced because those stricken with full-blown AIDS are often unable to work.

To curb this widespread problem, the government has embarked on a poverty reduction program that addresses not only the issue of heath, but also education, sanitation, and water. This five-year program was launched in November 2004, and a unified plan by the HIV/AIDS Prevention and Control Office (HAPCO) was drawn up to reduce the number of HIV infections and care for those affected by the disease. In 2004 HAPCO published and disseminated a thorough AIDS Monitoring and Evaluation Framework to analyze the prevalence of HIV/AIDS in Ethiopia. The HAPCO report revealed that although 90 percent of Ethiopians were aware of issues regarding HIV/AIDS, their willingness to change their behavioral patterns or sexual practices remained low. However, measures like condom distribution and establishing Voluntary Counseling and Testing (VCT) Centers—where people voluntarily test themselves for HIV and disclose their health status—as well as enforcing stricter controls for screening potential blood donors have met with slow but growing success. As of January 2005, an estimated 30,000 HIV-infected adults—including 35 percent of HIV-positive pregnant women and 9,000 people who have advanced AIDS infection—have been given antiretroviral drugs, which not only slow down the progression of the disease, but may reverse it as well.

A major challenge to Ethiopia's efforts to stem AIDS is the difficulty of implementing its plans effectively at all levels. Poor networking and coordination have resulted in a waste of valuable resources. In addition, the program is understaffed—there are about 20 health-care providers for every 100,000 inhabitants in Ethiopia—and relies heavily on free handouts. This could be a problem in the foreseeable future, when finances run low and such efforts are no longer sustainable.

RELIGION

ETHIOPIA IS HOME TO BOTH Christianity and Islam. In the southern regions, Muslim majorities predominate, representing 45 to 50 percent of the country's population. Christians, belonging mostly to the Ethiopian Orthodox Church, constitute 35 to 40 percent of Ethiopians. Closely related to the Coptic Church of Egypt, the Ethiopian Orthodox Church was founded in the fourth century, long before the arrival of European missionaries. The south also contains approximately 12 percent of animists.

Ethiopia's diverse religious tapestry has left a great legacy of art and architecture. Religious groups and organizations also play a vital role in Ethiopia's festivals, music, education, and cultural life.

CHRISTIANITY

The overwhelming majority of Ethiopia's Christians belong to the Ethiopian Orthodox Church, which has the allegiance of approximately 40 percent

There are about 90,000 Ethiopian Orthodox Christians in the Western Hemisphere, including a significant number of converts in the West Indies.

Left: **Ancient religious structures and paintings in Gondar, Axum, and Lalibela attract visitors from all over the world. Shown here is the façade of a Gondar church.**

Opposite: **A young Ethiopian Orthodox acolyte deep in prayer.**

The church's weekly services are the focal point for religious observance. Churches also conduct special services for religious holidays, which often include singing, dancing, and feasting. Saints' days are observed in addition to the regular Christian holidays.

of the country's people, among whom the Amhara and Tigray ethnic groups are particularly well represented. Today the church manages at least 20,000 parishes and employs about 290,000 clergy.

The roots of the Ethiopian Orthodox Church stretch back to ancient times. It was established in the fourth century A.D., when Christianity became the state religion of the Axumite kingdom. This occurred around the same time that Emperor Constantine made Christianity the official religion in Rome in 325 A.D. The church's influence soon became intertwined with that of the Ethiopian monarchy; so much so, that it remained the official state church in Ethiopia through to the era of Haile Selassie. As the church's traditions came directly from the Middle East, its version of Christianity differed from that spread by European missionaries in Africa later on. Drawing heavily on Old Testament traditions and scriptures, the Ethiopian Orthodox Church developed separately from Western Christianity.

The church's great power and influence in Ethiopian society remained intact for centuries. However, by the 1950s some educated Amharas and Tigrayans began to question the church's political and economic domination and its many privileges. After Haile Selassie was forced from

power, the Mengistu regime seized the land holdings of the church, divesting much of its power and imprisoning many of the religious leaders. While these measures altered the organization of the church, they did little to weaken the beliefs of its followers.

Members of the Ethiopian Orthodox Church believe in God and an array of angels and saints. Some church adherents blend Christian beliefs with traditional African beliefs, as is common in much of the continent. To demonstrate their faith, the laity are required to fast more than 200 days annually, including every Wednesday and Friday, and during Lent and Easter.

In contrast to most Christian churches in the West, Ethiopian Orthodox Churches are usually circular or octagonal in shape. Their interiors tend to be divided into three main parts. The outer ring is where most parishioners stay during church services; it also provides space for clergy to sing hymns and perform dances. The middle ring is designed for communion and is limited to those who have fully honored church precepts, such as the observance of fasts during designated days. The inner sanctum houses a sacred ark dedicated to the church's patron saint. This ark is retrieved by priests during religious ceremonies and is occasionally taken outside

Worshippers are usually expected to remove their shoes before entering an Ethiopian Orthodox Church. In some churches, women are not allowed to enter.

ORGANIZATION OF THE ETHIOPIAN ORTHODOX CHURCH

The Ethiopian Orthodox Church has long been characterized by well-defined hierarchies. At the top is the Abun (AH-boon), the venerable church patriarch whose all-encompassing leadership role is somewhat akin to the Archbishop of Canterbury in England. Originally, the selection of the Abun lay with leaders of Egypt's Coptic Church, but in 1950 the decision was handed over to the Episcopal Synod in Addis Ababa. Representing church authority on a regional basis are 32 bishops and archbishops *(the bishop of Axum is shown on the right)*.

Ethiopian Orthodox clergy are divided into three main categories. Deacons become qualified to assist with religious services after having studied for four years at a church-run school. The priesthood requires three or four years of additional study, and draws heavily on Ethiopian peasants to bolster its ranks. Priests are ranked according to their scholarly experience. The most specialized clergy are known as *debtera* (deb-ter-RAH). *Debtera* have received advanced training in areas such as musical performance, poetry, divination, and language studies. Besides these categories of clergy, the church utilizes the services of the laity.

for church processions. Only priests may enter the inner sanctum of an Ethiopian Orthodox Church.

Ethiopia is also home to about 500,000 Catholics, of whom approximately one-third adhere to the Ethiopian rite and two-thirds to the Latin rite. Ethiopia's Protestant denominations include the Fellowship of Evangelical Believers, Lutheran, Presbyterian, and Seventh-Day Adventist churches. The country also hosts branches of the Armenian Orthodox Church and the Greek Orthodox Church.

ISLAM

Practiced in Ethiopia for over 1,000 years, Islam is an all-encompassing religion that permeates the daily life of those who practice it. More than a religion, Islam is a culture and a way of life. It was first developed in Arabia in the seventh century, when the Prophet Muhammad claimed to have received the word of God—God being known as Allah in Islam—through a series of divine revelations. These revelations were later recorded in the Koran, the Muslim holy book. Muslims around the world over are required to practice Islam's five pillars of faith: (1) recitation of the *shahada*, proclaiming faith in Allah and Muhammad; (2) prayer five times daily; (3) almsgiving; (4) fasting during the month of Ramadan; and (5) making a pilgrimage to Mecca, which is regarded by Muslims to be the holiest city in the world.

Islam first spread to Ethiopia from the Arabian peninsula in the seventh century. Itinerant Muslim clerics from Arabia introduced their religion to the people along the coast first and then spread farther inland. These clerics initially spread their faith by encouraging Ethiopians to adapt Islam to their way of life, and the strategy bore fruit. By the 10th century, Islam was being adopted by the Afar people of the Denakil region. Eventually the ancient city of Harer became the center of Islamic culture in Ethiopia. Now home to more than 90 mosques and shrines, Harer was periodically used as a base from which the Muslims waged a series of holy wars against the Christian monarchy in the Ethiopian highlands.

A man reads the Koran. Muslims are found both in urban areas and in the countryside, but one contemporary observer has noted that the five pillars of Islam tend to be practiced more systematically in the cities.

"Of the two ways, that which is right; of the two decisions, that which is good—may just God lead you to follow."

—*A prayer used by Somali Muslims*

Relations between Ethiopia's imperial rulers and the region's Muslim population varied from outright warfare to mutual coexistence. Haile Selassie's government allowed Islamic courts to operate but discouraged the formation of Islamic schools. It did little to promote the teaching of Arabic, the religion's main language. When the Mengistu regime took power in the mid-1970s, it declared some Muslim holy days to be national holidays in an effort to promote greater religious freedom.

Islamic religious services are held in mosques and are usually attended by men only. Muslim women typically pray at home.

PILGRIMAGE TO THE TOMB OF SHEIKH HUSSEIN

Twice a year, thousands of Oromos converge at a site in the eastern foothills of the Bale Mountains to honor the 13th-century Muslim saint Sheikh Hussein. The first pilgrimage occurs from February to March to commemorate Sheikh Hussein's death; the second occurs from August to September to celebrate the anniversary of the Prophet Muhammad's birth. Each lasts approximately two weeks. Of the approximately 50,000 Oromos who participate in each pilgrimage, some will make the journey only once in their lives; others will return again and again.

Sheikh Hussein was an Islamic missionary from the Red Sea coast who spread Islam in the Ethiopian interior in the 13th century and won many converts and even more admirers. To keep the memory of Sheikh Hussein alive, his followers built a shrine in his honor in a town that bears his name. Originally, only Muslims made the pilgrimage to Sheikh Hussein's tomb. But, as the saint's teachings became more widely known over the centuries, other Oromos, who had not yet converted to Islam, began to join the pilgrimage. Those Oromos who undertake the pilgrimage today tend to blend Islam with traditional beliefs. Some of the pilgrims are devout Muslims, while others possess only a nominal faith.

Pilgrims come from all over the country to participate in the sacred journey, some coming from hundreds of miles away. Many people proceed to the shrine on foot; others ride mules, donkeys, or horses. During the journey—which can sometimes take months to complete—pilgrims are not allowed to cut their hair or sleep indoors. They traditionally carry forked walking sticks known as Oule Sheikh Hussein (OO-lay shake hoo-SANE) as they make their way to the holy site.

Once they arrive at the shrine, the pilgrims take turns entering Sheikh Hussein's tomb by crawling through a small doorway. What follows is an experience filled with mysticism and spiritual power. "The dark, still air of the tomb is charged with the body heat of the devotees who crowd in. Some circle the floor, praying, crying, chanting. Others, seemingly consumed by a transcendental passion, writhe and throw themselves about. Others, still half concealed in corners, in nooks and crannies, sit slumped, spellbound, and oblivious." (Graham Hancock, *African Ark*) While believers file inside the tomb, others remain outside to recite poetry, dance, and pray together. All of them hope that by visiting Sheikh Hussein's shrine, they will have both honored the memory of a great man and absorbed some of his ample goodness.

The most highly Islamicized ethnic group in Ethiopia today are the Somali; other Muslim peoples include the Afar and the Hareri. Significant numbers of the Oromo, Sidama, and Gurage populations practice Islam as well. Like their Christian neighbors, many Ethiopian Muslims blend their traditional beliefs with the precepts of the religion. Although the degree to which Ethiopians dilute Islam varies, their faith always revolves around the Sunni rather than the Shia branch of Islam.

A procession to make rain in Harer. In Ethiopia, traditional beliefs are strongest among the peoples living in the extreme southern and western portions of the country, since neither the Orthodox Church nor Islam penetrated these areas very thoroughly.

Villagers holding traditional beliefs often enlist the aid of spirit mediums, individuals who are perceived to have special powers to communicate with spirits and departed ancestors.

TRADITIONAL BELIEFS

Traditional belief systems differ from Islam and Christianity in important ways. For example, such belief systems do not revolve around sacred texts or holy books but are based on a set of accumulated values that has been passed down from generation to generation. Traditional belief systems also tend to incorporate a wide variety of gods and spirits, unlike either Islam or Christianity. The exact form that traditional beliefs take depends on the specific ethnic group in question.

Most people adhering to traditional beliefs have faith in a supreme God who is remote, but all-powerful. Spirits usually serve as intermediaries between people and the supreme God. Such spirits often take the form of natural phenomena such as mountains, water, caves, and trees. Some Ethiopians believe in protective spirits, known as *adbar* (AHD-bar) spirits, which are thought to govern the fortunes of communities. The female *adbar* is believed to offer protection against disease, poverty, and general misfortune, while the male *adbar* protects against war, conflict, and poor harvests. Evil spirits exist as well. In order to protect themselves against the evil *buda* (BOO-dah) spirit, some Ethiopians wear protective jewelry or call upon the services of specialized clergy known as *debtera* or a local wizard.

ETHIOPIA'S JEWS

Unlike other nations on the African continent, Ethiopia is home to an indigenous Jewish community, known as the Beta Israel people or the Falashas. Of the handful of Falashas who remain in Ethiopia today, most live near Lake Tana and in the highlands north of Gondar. Falasha men commonly work as blacksmiths, weavers, and tanners, while Falasha women are known for their skills in making pottery and baskets. These manual trades have traditionally been looked down upon by Amhara Christians. Falashas can often be found living in the same villages as Amharas, but in separate neighborhoods.

A Falasha girl wears a Star of David around her neck.

Like other Jews, the Falashas believe in one God, observe the Sabbath and most Jewish holidays, and circumcise their male children. They also follow strict laws concerning cleanliness and purity, such as that forbidding them from eating animals slaughtered by a non-Jew. The Falashas' holy book is the Torah, which is written in Ge'ez, not Hebrew. They do not use the Talmud, because this text was not codified until after the Falashas had established themselves in Ethiopia.

DIVERSITY CHARACTERIZES almost every aspect of Ethiopian society. Language is no exception. With more than 80 languages and over 200 dialects spoken within its borders, Ethiopia is, like many other countries on the African continent, a source of fascination to linguists. Amharic is the official language and was used for primary school instruction, but has been replaced in many areas by local languages since 1991. English is the most common foreign language and is taught in all secondary schools.

Above: **A priest presents a prayer book.**

Opposite: **An Ethiopian Orthodox priest reads Christian scriptures in Ge'ez, the liturgical language of the church.**

Other widely-spoken languages include Tigrinya, Oromo, and Somali. Given Ethiopia's linguistic complexity, the ability to speak more than one language is often a necessity. It is not surprising, then, that many Ethiopians are bilingual or multilingual.

Ethiopia's major languages belong to what linguists call the Afro-Asiatic family of languages. Afro-Asiatic languages spoken in Ethiopia are categorized into the Semitic, Cushitic, and Omotic groups. Approximately 12 Semitic languages are found in the country, including Amharic, Tigrinya, and Ge'ez (also called Ethiopic). Cushitic languages, of which there are approximately 22 in Ethiopia, include Oromo, Sidama, and Somali. Among the 18 or so Omotic languages spoken are Welayta and Kefa.

The other major language family found in Ethiopia is Nilo-Saharan. This language family, spoken by only 2 percent of Ethiopia's people,

Besides speaking their mother tongue, many Ethiopians can communicate in Amharic and English.

includes East Sudanic, Koman, Berta, and Kunama. Most of Ethiopia's Nilo-Saharan speakers live in the southwestern portion of the country near the border with Sudan.

AMHARIC

Amharic was the national language of Ethiopia during the imperial era—from the Solomonic dynasty in the 13th century to the fall of Emperor Haile Selassie in 1974—and has long been associated with courtly life and government. Its use by Ethiopian monarchs earned it the title Lesane Negest, which means language of kings. Derived from the ancient Ge'ez language in the Middle Ages, written Amharic became the official language of imperial correspondence during the reigns of Tewodros II

A Bible written in Amharic.

and Yohannes IV in the 19th century. Besides being the primary language of government and commerce, Amharic also served as the medium of instruction in Ethiopian primary schools until 1991.

Amharic has a more highly developed written tradition than most other languages used in Ethiopia. The Bible was first translated into Amharic in the early 19th century. Amharic writing became more widespread in the late 19th and early 20th centuries after Menelik II imported a printing press from Europe. Today, Amharic is spoken by 27 million of the country's population as a first language and between 7 to 15 million more speak it as a second language. Although Amharic is still the official language of Ethiopia, it is no longer promoted as the language of national unity as the FDRE recognizes the right of all peoples to use their own working languages. However, Amharic is still considered one of the country's most important means of communication. Amharic continues to play an important role in Addis Ababa. Studies have shown that native Amharic speakers have more education, better literacy skills, and greater employment rates in administrative and professional positions compared to non-Amharic speakers.

GE'EZ

Known as the classical language of Ethiopia, Ge'ez was brought to the Horn of Africa by Semitic peoples between 2000 B.C. and the beginning of the Christian era. Written Ge'ez first appeared around the fourth century A.D. Although it was Ethiopia's most important language for centuries, spoken Ge'ez was eventually displaced by Amharic around the 16th century. In the Middle Ages priests and monks translated Greek, Hebrew, and Arabic literary works into Ge'ez. The majority of these early texts dealt with theology, philosophy, law, and history. Perhaps the most famous Ge'ez text is entitled *Kibre Negest*, which means glory of kings. Written in the 14th century by Tigrayan priests, it chronicles and celebrates the reigns of early Ethiopian monarchs.

Although Ge'ez is no longer used in everyday spoken communication, it still finds a place in religious and educational settings. It is studied in some schools as a classical language. Ge'ez is still used by the Ethiopian Orthodox Church and is occasionally the language of choice for contemporary Ethiopian poets.

A priest presents the Bible. Christian scholars translated the Bible into Ge'ez shortly after Christianity became the official religion of the Ethiopian monarchy in the fourth century. Most Ge'ez literature is religious in character.

A young mother attends a literacy class. Ethiopian script is often written using a broad pen or a fine brush. Its symbols are characterized by thick vertical strokes and thin horizontal strokes.

WRITING SYSTEMS

The indigenous Ethiopian languages of Ge'ez, Amharic, and Tigrinya are written using a unique set of characters derived from an ancient writing system of South Arabia that used the Himyaritic alphabet. Ethiopian script contains 31 core characters that can be combined in various ways to form almost 200 more written characters. Since many characters in Ethiopia's writing system represent consonant-vowel combinations and thus form syllables, Ethiopian script is said to have a syllabary rather than an alphabet. The complexity of Ethiopia's writing system makes learning to read and write more difficult than it is in English. It also makes typing rather challenging!

Other writing systems are also used in Ethiopia. Arabic script is found in Ethiopia and is used not only for Arabic writing, but occasionally for Harari and Tigrinya as well. The Roman alphabet is used for writing English and other European languages. Its characters can also be used to write Ethiopian languages. In fact, Ethiopia's new government has encouraged the printing and publishing of written material in the Roman alphabet rather than the traditional Ethiopian script. A setback to this move is the high costs involved in republishing books

ETHIOPIAN PROVERBS

Proverbs capture human values in vivid and colorful ways. Sometimes, proverbs convey values common to many societies throughout the world; at other times, they reflect the distinct characteristics of a particular culture. The following are translations of some common Amharic and Oromo proverbs. When spoken in the original language, the proverbs often contain rhymes.

AMHARIC
- A guest is at first like gold, then later like silver, still later similar to common metal.
- The ear is not to be believed before the eye.
- Telling a secret to a babbler is like storing teff in a bag with holes in it.
- He who advises evil will be destroyed by it; he who digs a hole will fall into it.
- One who laughs at plowing time will cry at harvest time.
- Wood will not stand up against metal nor a lie against truth.
- A frog, having said, "I will become as big as an ox," blew herself up and burst.
- When spiderwebs unite, they can tie up a lion.

OROMO
- Indigestion is better than hunger.
- If you leave those who love you, you might go to those who hate you.
- Even if it is disagreeable, the word of an old man is never to be disdained.
- One's own cottage is better than somebody else's palace.
- He who knows much does not speak much.
- The hawk does not fly until its wings become strong.
- He who has money has relatives.

Although English is not commonly spoken as a mother tongue by Ethiopians, it is the medium of instruction in high school and university. It plays an important role in commerce, government, and international communication.

from traditional Ethiopian script to the Roman alphabet, especially for primary schools, where about twenty local languages are used as the medium of instruction. Ethiopia's printing houses are also too small and inadequately equipped to ensure the success of the government's plan to publish written materials in the Roman alphabet on a large scale.

The question many Ethiopians are asking is this: will the increased use of regional languages other than Amharic promote loyalty to the new federal government or will it encourage ethnic separatism? The answer is not yet clear.

THE CHALLENGES OF DIVERSITY

Ethiopia's multiplicity of languages has always made achieving national unity a challenge for the country's rulers. In the past the imperial government sought to promote such unity by mandating that Amharic be used as the primary language in Ethiopian schools, newspapers, and on radio and television. This policy sometimes caused non-Amharic speakers to feel discriminated against. When the Mengistu regime came to power in the 1970s it brought non-Amharic languages such as Oromo, Tigrinya, and Somali into radio broadcasts and literacy projects, but Amharic remained the language of government.

The current government is promoting the use of non-Amharic languages in keeping with its program of ethnic self-determination. The country's new administrative regions are largely organized on ethno-linguistic grounds. For example, the Tigray, Afar, Somali, and Oromo regions have declared their predominant languages to be the languages of regional government. This is the case even though their populations are not uniformly speakers of the main language. Some of the smaller regions in the southwest have opted to continue using Amharic.

LANGUAGE AND EDUCATION

Although instruction in Amharic was formerly required by the imperial regime, this is no longer the case in Ethiopian schools. The current government led by Meles Zenawi is seeking to introduce local languages as the means of instruction in primary schools as part of its effort to move away from Amharic dominance. Officials in Addis Ababa are also seeking to introduce English as a second language during the middle primary school years. In most high schools English remains the medium of instruction.

Falashas learning He-
brew.

Introducing local languages in schools to replace Amharic has not been easy. The new policy has required an enormous effort to plan, write, print, and distribute new curricular materials for use in the classrooms. Such material is needed for all subjects in grades one through six. A study done in 2003 on the use of language among high school students showed that most students were inclined to use a language that was deemed more effective and beneficial in maintaining network relations. Respondents indicated that they perceived Amharic and Oromo to be the most economically and socially prestigious of the languages used in Ethiopia. This could undermine the government's efforts to encourage a more ethnic-oriented policy toward languages. The new language policy has also dramatically reduced the pool of instructors qualified to teach in each region. In most cases only local residents can now teach in their region's schools because only they have an adequate knowledge of the provincial language. Students who do not speak the predominant language of their region sometimes feel that the new language policy is irrelevant to their needs.

Commenting on the confusion created by the new language policy in Ethiopian schools, one observer has written, "Change usually looks chaotic until the dust settles, and it has not yet settled in Ethiopia."

—Susan J. Hoben, Boston University

ARTS

ARTISTIC EXPRESSION IN ETHIOPIA has long been influenced by religious beliefs and practices. The Ethiopian Orthodox Church, for example, has contributed to the country's painting, architecture, and music for centuries. The icons that decorate Ethiopian illuminated manuscripts and churches of the Middle Ages are widely admired as one of the high points of Christian art. Ethiopian Muslims have a rich architectural tradition of their own. They are also known for crafting splendid pieces of ornate jewelry.

Religion continues to stimulate artistic expression today, but creativity in Ethiopia is not limited to churches, mosques, or sacred places. Secular art forms thrive in the country and are produced by both professional artists and ordinary people. The widespread existence of oral literature, arts and crafts, folk songs, and dances attests to the continued importance of the arts in the Ethiopian countryside today. Arts and crafts popular in Ethiopia include metalwork, leatherwork, basketry, weaving, and pottery. Some artisans use animal horns to make cups, shoehorns, lamps, vases, combs, and carvings.

Above: **Funerary sculptures.**

Opposite: **A minstrel plays the** *masenko,* **a traditional Ethiopian musical instrument.**

LITERATURE AND DRAMA

Ethiopia's oldest literary tradition is classical Ge'ez literature, the major works of which feature mostly religious and historical themes. One

**A performance in Addis
Ababa dramatizes Ethi-
opian Socialist ideals.**

example is *Hatata*, a treatise on God, reason, and human nature by
Zara Yaqob, a 17th-century theologist and philosopher from Axum. His
thoughts on the power of reason to explain human agonies have often
been compared to those of Descartes. More recent literature has dealt with
village life, tensions between city and countryside, and the relationship
between Christianity and traditional beliefs. Sahle Sellassie is a prominent
author whose works have been translated into English. Sellassie's books
include *Shinega's Village: Scenes of Ethiopian Life* (1964), *Warrior King*
(1974), and *Firebrands* (1979). Another well-known Ethiopian author is
Berhanu Zerihun.

Historical and religious themes have also featured prominently in
Ethiopian plays. One of Ethiopia's best-known dramatic works is *Oda
Oak Oracle* by poet laureate and playwright Tsegaye Gabre-Medhin. First
published in English in 1965, the play dramatizes the conflict between
superstition and reason in an Ethiopian setting. Gabre-Medhin died in

Yesterday's, Today's, and Tomorrow's Africa by Afewerk Tekle, one of Ethiopia's most celebrated artists. Afewerk Tekle's stained glass windows adorn Africa Hall in Addis Ababa.

February 2006. Ayalneh Mulatu, another leading contemporary playwright, has 24 full-length plays to his name, two of which were translated into English and Russian and three into Amharic. Mulatu has also staged musical drama, such as *Our Struggle, Unity,* and *Our Journey.*

VISUAL ARTS

Much of Ethiopia's early art was created to illustrate religious manuscripts or decorate churches. Many ancient churches seem like art galleries, filled with murals, frescoes, and colorful paintings depicting religious figures and symbols. Other early Ethiopian art was designed to pay tribute to national heroes and leaders. Artists usually painted these figures on wood, canvas, or parchment.

Commercial art began to develop in the 20th century during the reign of Haile Selassie. One popular piece of art depicts the Queen of Sheba's visit to King Solomon and is drawn in an animated, comic-strip style. Sometimes religious and commercial art can merge, as is evident in the popularity of paintings depicting Saint George, an important figure in Ethiopian Orthodox circles. Artists paint representations of Saint George

Ethiopia has many stories, folktales, and historical legends that are expressed orally rather than written down. Oral literary traditions are particularly common in southern and western Ethiopia and among ethnic Somalis.

on sheep and goat skins and then sell them to the public. Some artists paint designs on parchment, which is then used to make lampshades.

Well-known Ethiopian artists include Afewerk Tekle, Zerihun Yetmgeta, Gebre Kristos Desta, Skunder Boghossian, Lulseged Retta, and Wosene Worke Kosrof. In November 2002, a three-day art extravaganza organized by the International Conference on the History of Ethiopian Art was held in Addis Ababa to showcase Ethiopia's rich classical and contemporary artistic culture.

CHALLENGES FACING WOMEN ARTISTS

For centuries Ethiopian women have been expected to be wives and mothers first and forgo work beyond the household. Even today a woman's employment options outside of the home are limited. Due to family responsibilities and financial hardship, formal female education has been deemphasized, so women have been prevented from competing in spheres dominated by men, such as government and business. The same is true for professional art.

The number of Ethiopian women artists is still relatively small. Women make up only a small proportion of students at the University School of Fine Art and Design in Addis Ababa, and are underrepresented in national exhibitions. Some aspiring female artists apply to study overseas, but find scholarships hard to come by.

Most of the women artists working professionally in Ethiopia today received their training at the University School of Fine Art and Design. Some work as illustrators for newspapers, while others work at the University School or teach art in the primary and secondary schools.

Desta Hagos is one of the most prominent female artists in Ethiopia today. She has displayed her paintings at a number of solo exhibitions.

Trained at the University School of Fine Art and Design in the 1960s, Desta is best known for her paintings depicting the natural environment.

Another well-known Ethiopian artist is Katsala Atenafu, the first woman to enroll at the University School of Fine Art and Design. After graduating from the school in 1964, Katsala specialized in handicrafts, particularly weaving. She now works at the Ethiopian Handicrafts Center, which trains people to make rugs, textiles, baskets, and pottery.

The artwork produced by Ethiopian women comes in a variety of styles and genres. Many artists paint scenes of women at work: baking, grinding grain, weaving cloth, or carrying firewood or heavy water jugs. In these works, the message conveyed about the hard life of Ethiopian women is unmistakable. Women artists are also known for painting portraits and nature scenes. Their works vary from realistic to abstract, somber to upbeat. Painting is perhaps the most common art form (in watercolors and oil), but women also produce woodcuts, sketches, collages, sculptures, and tapestries. Despite considerable obstacles, women artists in Ethiopia remain determined to express themselves and to create.

Women's contributions to the craft industry are particularly notable in the production of the *mesob* (a basket-like food table) and in carpet weaving and pottery.

ARTS AND CRAFTS

A large proportion of Ethiopian metalwork springs from the country's religious traditions. Ethiopian Muslims have earned a reputation for producing lovely silver work with geometric patterns and designs that are typical of Islamic art. Most common are decorative pieces of jewelry, such as bracelets, pins, and charm boxes. Metalwork is also prized among the Oromo ethnic group. Oromo women enjoy wearing silver necklaces on which they fasten old European coins for decoration.

Handcrafted silver bracelets for sale in Kefa.

Leatherwork is another thriving handicraft industry in Ethiopia because of the country's ample supply of livestock. Belts, bags, and sandals are among the most common items produced and sold. The Afar people use leather to make curved sheaths for their knives; people in the Bale region are known for making fine leather saddles. The *agilgil* (ah-GEHL-gil) is a popular handicraft that combines leatherwork with basketry. Found among highland societies, this item is a special leather-covered basket used to carry food.

Basketry thrives in many areas of Ethiopia but is particularly well established in Harer. Skilled artisans use local grasses to make baskets and often decorate the finished product with colorful designs. The *mesob* (meh-SOHB) is probably the largest type of basket produced in the

USING THE BODY AS A CANVAS

What happens when art, fashion, and tremendous creativity are combined? Among the Surma people, the answer is body painting. Based in the mountains of southwestern Ethiopia, the Surma are a seminomadic people who raise cattle and grow crops for a living. Surma men are known for conducting fierce stick fighting competitions, while the women are renowned for adorning themselves with lip plates. The Surma's rich tradition of body painting, however, may be their most fascinating custom of all.

The Surma's prime body painting season comes after the October harvest, when people have sufficient leisure time to devote to their art. No one is left out; men and women, young and old, are encouraged to paint and be painted. Before a person is painted, their body is covered with a mixture of chalk and water. Patterns are then created by someone who removes part of the chalky mixture with their fingertips. The only limit to the designs is in the painter's imagination. Patterns can be vertical, horizontal, diagonal, circular, or any combination thereof. Some patterns are designed to attract the opposite sex, while others might be used to scare away potential enemies. Paintings on the face can resemble a mask or a series of multicolored stars. Surma children have been known to paint one another as if they were twins.

The Surma are not the only Ethiopian people to use body painting as a form of adornment. The Karo of the lower Omo River region *(shown above)* also paint one another. Sometimes they paint multicolored, masklike patterns on their faces or patterns that imitate the spots of the guinea fowl.

country; it often serves as a table in Ethiopian homes and can be seen in Ethiopian restaurants around the world. Like baskets, woven items are also produced for domestic use and find their way into local markets. Heavy blankets, light cotton cloth, woolen caps, and rugs are among the most common woven goods. Pottery is also another of Ethiopia's crafts.

Household goods such as jars, dishes, bowls, cooking pots, and water jugs are needed for their practical value, while flowerpots, planters, and ashtrays are produced for the tourist market.

SONG AND DANCE

Ethiopian music reflects both African and Middle Eastern influences but retains a character of its own. Early music was highly religious in character. One of the first known Ethiopian composers was Saint Yared, a sixth-century musician who wrote songs for the Ethiopian Orthodox Church. Today musical chants still form an important part of church services in the Ethiopian Orthodox Church, and religious schools offer training to students wishing to study church hymns, dances, and chants.

Folk music remains very much a part of life in the Ethiopian countryside. Ethiopian minstrels, known locally as *azmari* (az-MAHR-ee), help villagers mark important events by performing at weddings, festivals, and funerals. These minstrels play traditional instruments and act as a catalyst for community participation in musical performances. Although Ethiopia's many ethnic groups have developed their own distinctive styles of song and dance, some kinds of music are common to a number of groups. Folk songs are a common vehicle for expressing political sentiments.

There are a number of musical instruments unique to Ethiopia that give folk music there its distinctive sound. Stringed instruments include two kinds of harps, the *bagana* (beh-geh-NAH) and the *kerar* (kuh-RAHR), and a fiddle-like instrument known as the *masenko* (mah-SEEN-koh). The *meleket* (MAH-leh-ket) is a wooden wind instrument, and the *washint* (WAH-shint) is a bamboo flute. The most common percussion instruments are the *kebero* (KEH-beh-roh), a rattle, and the *atamo* (ah-TAH-moh), a drum. Some popular Ethiopian singers are Aster Aweke, known as Africa's

Aretha Franklin, and traditional folk singer Damtew Ayele. Ejigayehu Shibabaw, more popularly known as Gigi, made waves with her 2001 album titled *Gigi* for its exciting fusion of contemporary and traditional music styles. Her second album, *Gold and Wax*, was launched in 2006 to critical acclaim. Another musician fusing jazz and Latin influences with traditional style is Mulatu Astatke, also known as the "Father of Ethiopian Jazz."

Although dance in Ethiopia varies by region, it regularly brings members of the opposite sex together for celebration and courtship. The Somalis in the Ogaden engage in special dances following the rainy season. Men wearing white robes serenade eligible women and jump high in the air to show their strength. Women in colorful gowns clap and join in the dancing to the accompaniment of drums. Karo men and women engage in a special seduction dance that often leads to marriage. Men standing in a line jump in unison toward the women, who then come forward to choose their partners.

A drummer performs for Timkat celebrations in Lalibela. Much of Ethiopia's music today centers around religious services and festivals.

LEISURE

ETHIOPIANS LIKE TO PLAY, RELAX, and entertain themselves, but as many people are busy earning a living and making sure that their families are fed, clothed, and housed, they have relatively little time for leisure activities. The country's droughts, famines, and warfare have also seriously eroded people's opportunities to enjoy leisure time.

Recreational pursuits in Ethiopia do not usually require high-powered technology or expensive equipment. Sporting equipment often needs to be imported and is thus too expensive for the average Ethiopian. Given these circumstances, it is not surprising that soccer and distance running are among Ethiopia's most popular sports. Addis Ababa boasts fine athletic facilities, restaurants, local bars (which the locals call *buna bet*, meaning coffeehouse), movie theaters, and parks, but most rural Ethiopians go without these things and still try to enjoy life.

Ethiopia's close ties with the Soviet Union in the 1970s and 1980s brought with it athletic as well as diplomatic perquisites. Eager to reward the Mengistu regime for its loyal support, the Soviets donated sporting goods to the country's athletic organizations and paid for Ethiopian athletes to participate in competitions in the Soviet Union.

Left: **Cinema-goers browse through a list of movies shown at a movie theater.**

Opposite: **A gigantic billboard features long-distance runner Haile Gebreselassie in Addis Ababa. Ethiopia is renowned for producing world champions in the field of competitive running.**

If one took a poll asking Ethiopians to name their favorite sport, soccer would probably top the list.

On Ethiopian soccer, The World Encyclopedia of Soccer *says this:"Before the rise of sub-Saharan soccer-playing countries in the mid-1960s, no country on the African continent was more respected for its contribution to the game's growth, and there were few who were able to match wits with the skill and determination of Ethiopian players."*

POPULAR SPORTS

Ethiopia is considered a pioneer of African soccer. The sport was introduced to the country in the 1920s and 1930s, primarily by the Italians. Ethiopians launched their first soccer club, the Saint George Sports Association, in 1935 and established the Ethiopian Football Federation eight years later. After entering international competitions in the late 1940s, Ethiopia launched the African Football Confederation with Egypt and Sudan in 1956. These three nations competed in the first Africa Cup in Khartoum in 1957. Ethiopia celebrated in January 1962, when its national team defeated Egypt 4–2 in overtime to win the Africa Cup in Addis Ababa. Among the thousands of adoring fans witnessing the great victory was Emperor Haile Selassie.

Today soccer is popular all over Ethiopia. National tournaments are regularly held in Addis Ababa. The Africa Cup competition, which is hosted occasionally by the capital, draws large crowds to the 30,000-seat Addis Ababa Stadium. International soccer matches are broadcast frequently on Ethiopian television and are very popular, especially the World Cup. Ethiopia itself is a regular at the FIFA World Cup qualifiers, entering its first qualifiers match in 1962. Although Ethiopia has never advanced past the competition qualifiers to the final round, it did have its best moment in 1983, when it defeated Djibouti 8–1.

The Olympic games have attracted many talented Ethiopian athletes, particularly distance runners. The high altitude in many parts of Ethiopia provides an ideal training ground for runners, just as it does in neighboring Kenya, which has also produced world-class runners. Ethiopian athletes might have won more gold medals had it not been for their participation in the Olympic boycotts of 1976 and 1984.

In the 1992 summer games in Barcelona, Ethiopia earned three medals, placing fourth among African nations competing. Making history that

OLYMPIC HEROES FROM THE PAST

At the beginning of the 1960 summer games in Rome, Abebe Bikila was a little-known member of Haile Selassie's Imperial Guard. When the games were over, Abebe had become the greatest sports hero Ethiopia had ever known. His first place finish in the marathon garnered world attention because he had run the streets of Rome barefoot. Not only was he the first person from black Africa to win an Olympic gold medal, Abebe would be the first to win the Olympic marathon twice. He won the 1964 Olympic marathon just six weeks after his appendix was removed; his time set world and Olympic records.

Abebe's Olympic triumphs made him a hero to African sports fans all over the continent. He inspired a whole generation of Ethiopian runners, and his name became synonymous with speed and stamina. He died in 1973 at the age of 41, seven years after becoming paralyzed in a near-fatal auto accident. His funeral in Addis Ababa drew thousands of fans and admirers.

Mamo Wolde won the marathon at the 1968 summer games in Mexico City, continuing where his teammate Abebe Bikila left off four years earlier. Mamo also earned a silver medal in the 10,000 meter (6.21 mile) run at Mexico City and took home a bronze in the marathon during the 1972 summer games in Munich. Despite coming in third in the marathon in 1972, Mamo's time that year was five minutes under his gold medal-winning time in the 1968 games.

Miruts Yifter won the bronze in the 10,000 meter run at the 1972 Olympics, and earned two golds in Moscow eight years later in the 5,000 (3.1 mile) and 10,000 meter races. His time in the 5,000 meter run in 1980 was then the second fastest in Olympic history.

year was Derartu Tulu, who won the 10,000 meter race and thus became the first Ethiopian woman to bring home a gold. Besides Derartu's gold medal, Ethiopia picked up two bronze medals in Barcelona, thanks to Fita Bayisa's third place finish in the men's 5,000 meter run and Addis Abebe's effort in the men's 10,000 meter race. Currently there are two Ethiopian long-distance Olympic and world champions. Haile Gebreselassie, known affectionately as Jegnaw (fearless hero) by Ethiopians, has broken more than 10 world records and has brought home the gold for the 10,000 meter race in both the 1996 Atlanta and 2000 Sydney Olympics. Kenenisa Bekele, another Ethiopian hero, won the gold for the 10,000 meter race and silver for the 5,000 meter race at the 2004 Athens Olympics.

Ethiopians also participate in basketball, volleyball, tennis, boxing, swimming, and bicycle racing, particularly in urban areas. Most of the

Abebe Bikila's stunning performance in the marathon at the Rome Olympics in 1960 marked the first time that a gold medal was awarded to a competitor from black Africa. Coincidentally, that year is considered the year of African independence, because 14 African nations broke free from European colonial rule.

Women smoking a pipe. Ethiopian women generally have less leisure time than men and are usually burdened with heavy child care and housekeeping responsibilities.

competitors in these pastimes, however, are men. Female participation in sports is not as common in Ethiopia—or in Africa as a whole—as it is in the West. Sports have traditionally been viewed as masculine forms of recreation, whereas other leisure pursuits such as singing, visiting friends, or engaging in arts and crafts are less rigidly defined by gender.

SPORTS UNIQUE TO ETHIOPIA

Afar men play a game called *kwosso* (KWOH-soh), a kind of keep-away game in which two teams vie to keep possession of a goatskin ball. The game is very fast-paced and is played on the hard, sandy desert plain near the Denakil Depression. Sometimes, as many as 200 men play at one time. *Kwosso* features frequent tackling and collisions. Injuries occur as players collide and attempt to strip their opponents of the ball. Contestants

Some Ethiopian men stage war games on horseback as a form of recreation.

wear no protective padding and are usually clad only in loincloths because of the intense desert heat. Games can last an entire day.

In *feres gugs* (FAIR-es googs), players on opposing teams mount horses and carry lightweight wooden staffs. Those on offense try to strike the opposing players with their staffs, either by throwing the staffs or by direct contact. Those on defense ward off blows with shields made of hippopotamus or rhinoceros hide and dodge attacks by maneuvering their horses.

GAMES PEOPLE PLAY

Ethiopian adults enjoy games of both skill and chance. Besides cards and chess, Ethiopians play a board game known as *gabata* (geh-beh-TAH). Similar games are played in much of the rest of the continent under different names. In this game, players place seeds in depressions on a wooden game board and then try to capture the seeds of their opponents. Potential moves are governed by complex rules. The player who captures the most seeds wins the game—and often the money that has been bet on the contest beforehand. *Gabata* is also known as *wari-solo*, *mancala*, or *congkak* in different cultures around the world.

YOUTH RECREATION

One popular form of recreation for Ethiopian children is listening to folktales, which often feature animals as the main characters. A popular theme is the value of generosity over greed.

Children in Ethiopia have invented their own traditional games. *Debebekosh* (deh-BEH-beh-kosh), for example, is the Ethiopian form of hide and seek; *kelelebosh* (keh-LEH-leh-kosh) is Ethiopia's version of jacks. Surma children enjoy participating in the snake dance, in which they squat on the ground and hold onto each other's shoulders, hopping and forming a snakelike pattern on the ground. As they move forward in the slithering procession, the children sing in happy voices.

Youth soccer is popular in both the cities and the countryside. Another sport popular in rural areas is known as *ganna* (gehn-NAH) and resembles field hockey. Urban high schools tend to field teams in volleyball, soccer, gymnastics, and basketball.

Schoolchildren enjoy their free time.

Boys living in Ethiopian cities sometimes raise pigeons as a form of recreation.

FESTIVALS

HOLIDAYS IN ETHIOPIA provide an opportunity to participate in an array of leisure activities for people who ordinarily have little time for recreational pursuits. The festivals accompanying many Ethiopian holidays involve young and old, women and men, rich and poor, and town and countryside. Although each festival has its unique history and purpose, they bring Ethiopians together. Feasting, visiting family and friends, giving gifts, singing and dancing, participating in parades, and playing games are just some of the activities that make Ethiopian holidays so popular.

Most Ethiopian festivals are religious in character. Many are tied to the Ethiopian Orthodox Church, which holds special services, ceremonies, and processions during the most important Christian holidays. Although Christian holidays dominate the official Ethiopian calendar, other religious groups have special celebrations that are held throughout the year as well. Ethiopian Muslims observe the holy month of Ramadan, during which they fast between daybreak and sundown. Ethiopians holding traditional beliefs celebrate the change of seasons, harvests, and rites of passage such as birthdays and weddings.

Whatever their religious convictions, Ethiopians observe holidays according to a unique calendar. Unlike the Gregorian calendar, which is used almost everywhere in the world, the Julian calendar used in Ethiopia divides the year into 13 months. The first 12 months have 30 days each, while the 13th month has five days, unless it is a leap year, during which it has six. The first day of the Ethiopian year falls on September 11.

GANNA

Ganna (gehn-NAH), the Ethiopian Christmas, is celebrated on January 7. Church services marking the sacred day often begin as early as 3 A.M. In Addis Ababa, Ganna services are held at the Church of the Nativity and

Opposite: **A man takes a rest from celebrating the festival of Maskal at Debre Sina.**

113

A festival honoring Saint Gebre Menfes Kiddus takes place annually atop a mountain outside of Addis Ababa. Gebre Menfes Kiddus established a monastery there, and, to honor him, priests lead processions to the mountain with their tabots, crosses, and parasols in hand. The subsequent ceremonies draw large crowds every year.

at Trinity Cathedral, where robed priests carrying prayer staffs officiate. They begin by leading hymns and then conduct Mass, assisted by poets, singers, and drummers. After the service ends at approximately 9 A.M., worshippers return home to mark the occasion with special meals. A ball game also called *ganna* is played in the late afternoon and is an essential part of the day's festivities. Resembling field hockey, *ganna* is played by men and older boys, who compete until nightfall. In the evenings celebrations continue as people exchange gifts and enjoy refreshments.

TIMKAT

Timkat (TIM-keht), also known as the Feast of Epiphany, is the most important religious festival in Ethiopia. The holiday officially falls on

MAJOR ETHIOPIAN HOLIDAYS

January 7	Ganna (Christmas)
January 10	Eid al-Adha (end of the Hajj Pilgrimage to Mecca)
January 19	Timkat (Feast of Epiphany)
March 2	Victory of Adwa commemoration
March/April	Good Friday and Easter
April 6	Ethiopian Patriots Day
April 10	Mawlid (Birth of the Prophet Muhammad)
May 1	Labor Day
May 28	National Day
August 21	Buhe
September 11	Enkutatash (New Year)
September 27	Maskal (Finding of the True Cross)
December 28	Kullubi (Feast of Saint Gabriel)
(date varies)	Eid al-Fitr (end of fasting month for Ramadan)

A Timkat procession emerges from a rock-hewn church.

January 19, two weeks after the Ethiopian Christmas, and commemorates the baptism of Jesus. Organized celebrations last three days and include processions on Timkat Eve, the commemoration of the baptism of Christ, and the Feast of Saint Michael, an Ethiopian saint. Ethiopian families observe Timkat by brewing beer, baking bread, and feasting on lamb. New clothes are brought out and children are given gifts. All of this takes place beneath the clear and sunny skies of the dry season.

Formal Timkat celebrations begin with church-led processions and all-night prayer vigils. On Timkat Eve, priests remove the *tabot* (TAH-boht), a symbol of the Ark of the Covenant, from their churches and carry it in a procession, making sure that it is covered with an ornate cloth at all times. The processions are led by church leaders carrying sacred relics such as Bibles, crosses, and silver canes. In Addis Ababa, the procession ends up at the old race course known as Jan Medha, where an all-night prayer vigil is held. At a special sunrise service the next morning, an elder of the Ethiopian Orthodox Church presides over a ceremony commemorating Christ's baptism. He dips a cross and a burning candle into some water, then sprinkles the liquid onto the crowd of worshippers. The assembled priests then carry their *tabots* back to their respective churches in another impressive procession.

The events occurring on Timkat day draw thousands of participants and spectators onto the streets. Ceremonies and parades are held all over Ethiopia to mark the festive occasion. Shaded by bright parasols, dignitaries and church elders listen to speeches, while others read passages from the Bible before the faithful. The head of the Ethiopian Orthodox Church, the Abun, usually attends Timkat ceremonies in Addis Ababa, wearing colorful robes befitting his position. Church attendants carry Bibles and crosses in the outdoor procession and wear glittering, jewel-covered capes and robes of velvet and satin.

ENKUTATASH

The Ethiopian New Year is celebrated on September 11, at the end of the rainy season. New Year's Day is called Enkutatash (en-koo-TAH-tahsh), meaning gift of jewels, to commemorate the Queen of Sheba's return to Ethiopia after visiting King Solomon, upon which she was given precious jewelry. Today the holiday is marked by the lighting of fires on New Year's Eve. The most important celebration is held at Kostete

During Timkat some white-robed priests chant and dance while carrying their rattles and silver-tipped staffs. They are often joined in the procession by young boys carrying bells or flags.

Yohannes Church in the Gondar region. There, three days of prayers, processions, and services mark the advent of the New Year. In Addis Ababa the biggest celebration is held at Raguel Church on Entoto Mountain. The most pious adherents of the Ethiopian Orthodox tradition observe the Feast of Saint John the Baptist; others simply exchange greetings or cards to mark the New Year.

MASKAL

Both a secular and a religious holiday, Maskal (mehs-KEHL) is held annually on September 27, two weeks after the Ethiopian New Year. The holiday celebrates the coming of spring as well as the discovery of the True Cross of Christ, which is the cross upon which Jesus was crucified. According to legend, the True Cross of Christ was found by Saint Helena, mother of Constantine the Great, in the fourth century. Later, a relic of the True Cross was given to Ethiopia's kings to reward them for protecting Coptic Christians in their country. Maskal has been celebrated in Ethiopia for more than 1,600 years.

Festivities associated with Maskal include dancing, feasting, parades, gun salutes, and the setting of bonfires. In Addis Ababa an elaborate holiday procession goes from Africa Hall and Jubilee Palace to Maskal Square. Approximately 100,000 people come to watch the parade each year, which features bands, finely-decorated floats, and the participation of priests, scouts, civic groups, soldiers, and schoolchildren. Some priests wear white turbans and robes, while others are clad in more colorful garb, including bright caps and flowing capes. Many bring with them ornate bronze crosses, sometimes mounted on poles or worn as pendants. Children participate in the parade by singing and dancing to the accompaniment of drums. At sunset, the assembled crowd watches

Buhe (BOO-hay) is an Ethiopian holiday resembling Halloween and occurs each August 21. On that night, groups of boys go from house to house singing songs until they are given handfuls of bread to eat. In the cities boys who perform at people's doorsteps are given money.

Celebrants in Axum prepare to light a bonfire to celebrate the festival of Maskal.

participants throw torches onto a tall bonfire, which burns all night. This ceremony is observed not only in the capital, but in most town squares and village marketplaces throughout the country.

KULLUBI

Kullubi (koo-LOO-bee), one of the most popular festivals, honors Saint Gabriel, a patron saint for many Orthodox Christians. Viewed as a great protector and miracle worker, he is honored with special celebrations all over the country on December 28. Those eager to pay tribute to the saint make a pilgrimage to Saint Gabriel's church in Kullubi, located in the Harer region 40 miles (64 km) from Dire Dawa. Some of the faithful arrive by car; others find seats on buses or trucks; still others ride mules. Many of the pilgrims walk to the site.

Eventually about 100,000 people converge on Kullubi. The pilgrims' primary goal while at Kullubi is to make vows and give thanks to Saint Gabriel. Those who can, crowd into the church for Mass; those left outside listen to services broadcast over loudspeakers. Some pilgrims also bring their babies to be baptized. In fact, during the three-day celebration at Kullubi, approximately 1,000 babies are baptized, and many are named after the saint their parents have come to honor.

ISLAMIC HOLIDAYS

EID AL-ADHA This festival is celebrated by Muslims on the tenth day of Dhul Hijja, the twelfth and final month of the Islamic calendar. It commemorates the willingness of the Prophet Ibrahim to sacrifice his son Ishmael for Allah. Eid al-Adha (EED AHL-ad-ah) is celebrated to mark the end of the hajj, which is a pilgrimage to Mecca. Every able-bodied Muslim who can afford the pilgrimage to Mecca is encouraged to do so at least once in his lifetime. Pilgrims to Mecca dress in simple white unhemmed clothing and perform a series of ritualistic acts symbolic of the lives of Ibrahim and his wife, Hajarah. Some of the rituals include circling around the Ka'abah, the House of Allah, in a counterclockwise direction and walking seven times back and forth between the hills of Safa and Marwah.

A short prayer followed by a sermon giving thanks to Allah starts off the celebration of Eid al-Adha. Muslims who can afford to sacrifice domesticated animals such as goats, sheep, or cows are encouraged to do so. The sacrifice, called Qurban (KOOR-bahn), is then equally divided among family members and the needy.

EID AL-FITR The name of this festival means the day that returns often, and it is celebrated during the ninth month of the Islamic calendar. This celebration marks the end of Ramadan, a month when Muslims fast from dawn to dusk. This festival of cheer, like Eid al-Adha, usually begins with devotees attending special prayers and a short sermon performed in mosques, squares, or any available open areas. In Ethiopia these prayer services are usually held in urban centers rather than in smaller towns and villages. After the prayers, Muslims will don new clothes and visit their friends and relatives. Eid al-Fitr (EED AHL-fitr) is a day of forgiveness, brotherhood, piety, and reflection for the grace, strength, and self-control Allah has given followers of the faith during the fasting month.

FOOD

TWO WORDS ARE KEY to understanding Ethiopian cuisine: hot and spicy. Many herbs and spices are used to give Ethiopian food its fiery flavor, but perhaps the most essential ingredient is *berbere* (ber-BER-ray), a hot pepper sauce common in many Ethiopian dishes. First-time tasters may find foods spiced with *berbere* truly scorching, but Ethiopians would not think of having a meal without it. *Berbere* is a particularly important ingredient in *wat* (weht), a type of spicy stew that is the country's most popular dish.

Besides enjoying spicier food than most Westerners are accustomed to, Ethiopians are less prone to take food for granted. Many families struggle to put enough food on the table and are ever conscious of the specters of drought and famine that have taken such a toll in the past. Ethiopia continues to depend on food imports to feed its people.

Left: **A relief worker feeds children during a famine. Food shortages are a continuing concern because of irregular rainfall, a decline in productive agricultural land, and the fast-growing population.**

Opposite: **A woman prepares traditional Ethiopian doughnuts in Gambela.**

121

Cooking *injera* (in-JAIR-ah), Ethiopian bread. Rural women usually cook their family's meals over an open fire; urban women may have a kerosene stove over which to cook. Electric ones are found only in the wealthiest urban homes.

Most cooking is done by women. Rural women probably spend more time on cooking than on any other task.

COOKING, ETHIOPIAN STYLE

Most rural Ethiopians supply their own food, either by growing grains, fruit, or vegetables or by raising chickens, goats, sheep, or cattle. Although Ethiopians in the countryside often go to the market to obtain certain spices or specialty food items, they rarely have the chance to shop in large grocery stores. Such supermarkets exist only in large urban areas such as Addis Ababa. Only small numbers of Ethiopians have access to frozen and convenience foods, and relatively few have kitchen appliances such as refrigerators, electric stoves, or toasters. Food preparation is much more time consuming and labor intensive in Ethiopia than it is in the West.

Meal preparation typically involves gathering wood for the cooking fire, grinding grain, pounding and mixing spices, baking, carrying water, washing and cutting vegetables, and much more. Despite the complexity of many of their dishes, Ethiopian women do not typically use written recipes when cooking. Instead, culinary practices are passed from one generation to the other through example and instruction.

POPULAR DISHES

Ethiopia's national dish is *wat*, a type of stew with a rich and spicy sauce, which usually contains salt, garlic, ginger, black pepper, cardamon, onion, lemon juice, nutmeg, wine, water, spiced butter, paprika, fenugreek seeds, and *berbere*. The most popular form of *wat*, *doro wat* (DOR-oh weht), contains chicken. However, *wat* can also contain beef, lamb, fish, or vegetables. Vegetarian *wat*, based on lentils, beans, or chickpeas, is eaten by members of the Orthodox Church on fasting days.

A traditional Ethiopian meal includes a selection of *wats* served on *injera*. The meal is laid out on a *mesob*, a traditional Ethiopian basket used as a table.

The most important side dish in Ethiopian meals is *injera*, a special kind of bread made from teff, an Ethiopian grain. When preparing *injera*, Ethiopian women first hand-grind teff grain to make flour. Next they make the batter by combining the flour with water and letting the mixture ferment for three or four days. Then they pour the fermented batter in a circular pattern onto a clay griddle over a fire. Cooking only takes a few minutes. The finished product is a thin, pancake-shaped bread with little pits created by fermentation bubbles. It has a mild, slightly sour taste and a spongy, limp texture. During mealtimes, *injera* is kept in a covered basket beside the main dish. Diners use the bread to scoop up food and absorb spicy sauces.

As a rule, Ethiopians do not consume nearly as much meat as Westerners. When a meal does call for meat, chicken, beef, or lamb are the most common choices; in the dry lowland regions, people sometimes eat goat or camel meat. *Kitfo* (KIT-foh) is a popular dish made with raw chopped beef and spices. The first step in making *kitfo* is to sauté onions, green peppers, chilies, ginger, garlic, and cardamon in spiced butter. Once this is done, lemon juice, *berbere*, salt, and raw beef are added. The finished *kitfo* can be an appetizer or a main dish and is often served in green peppers or with *injera*.

A greengrocer in Addis Ababa. Fruits and vegetables are staples of the Ethiopian diet.

Alecha *(ah-LEH-chah) is a milder stew than* wat. *It contains chicken or beef, combined with onions, potatoes, carrots, cabbage, green peppers, chilies, garlic, turmeric, ginger, black pepper, and salt.*

Dried beef is commonly eaten in rural areas. The meat is cut into strips, cured with salt, pepper, and *berbere*, and hung out to dry in a cool place for approximately two weeks. It is then eaten as a snack.

One of Ethiopia's most popular vegetarian meals is *yataklete kilkil* (yah-TAH-kelt KIL-i-kil), a casserole of fresh vegetables flavored with garlic and ginger. It is served as a main dish during Lent and as a side dish at other times of the year. Typical ingredients for *yataklete kilkil*, besides garlic and ginger, include potatoes, broccoli, carrots, green beans, onions, cauliflower, green pepper, hot chilies, salt, pepper, and scallions. This meal is traditionally served with *injera* or rice. *Yemiser selatta* (yeh-mis-SIR seh-LAH-tah) is another vegetarian favorite. This is a lentil-based salad with shallots and chilies, commonly served during Lent.

Although *injera* is the most popular accompaniment to Ethiopian meals, a number of other side dishes are commonly served throughout

THE SPICE OF LIFE

It would be hard to imagine Ethiopian food without spices. They are an essential ingredient of the country's most popular dish, *wat*, and give countless other dishes their flavor and heat. Among Ethiopia's most commonly used spices are pepper, garlic, bishop's weed, rue, mint, cloves, cinnamon, turmeric, and nutmeg.

Several of these spices are combined with powerful peppers, herbs, and water to

form *berbere*, the favorite hot sauce of Ethiopians. *Berbere* is a key ingredient in beef and chicken stews and is used as a dip for raw meat dishes. The exact ingredients used to make *berbere* form a long list: paprika, red pepper, salt, ginger, onion, garlic, cloves, cinnamon, nutmeg, cardamon, allspice, black pepper, fenugreek, coriander, red wine, water, vegetable oil, cumin, and turmeric. These items are mixed and heated to form a zesty sauce as hot as fire.

The famous South African author Laurens van der Post tried *berbere* on one of his early trips to Ethiopia. When his hosts offered him raw meat dipped in *berbere* sauce, van der Post decided to be adventurous. "If one must eat meat raw," he recalled later, "it is surely best done in this way, for the sauce gives the impression of being hot enough to cook the meat right on the tongue."

the country as well. *Dabo kolo* (DAH-boh KOH-loh) is a roasted cookie made with wheat flour, *berbere*, sugar, and salt. It makes for a crunchy, spicy snack. *Yeshimbra assa* (yeh-shim-BRAH AH-sa) is the name for fish-shaped snacks made from chickpea flour. Ground chickpeas, oil, onions, *berbere*, salt and pepper are mixed and formed into a paste. They are then molded into fish shapes and fried. For dessert, Ethiopians sometimes serve strawberries; stalks of sugarcane are also chewed as sweet snacks.

A special butter is used widely as a spread and in cooking. This spicy butter, known as *niter kebbeh* (NIT-er ki-BAY), is made from butter, onions, garlic, ginger, turmeric, cardamon, cinnamon, cloves, and nutmeg. It is an essential ingredient in *wat*.

BEVERAGES

Ethiopian cups and glasses are usually filled with milk, beer, wine, tea, or coffee. Milk is traditionally a children's beverage and can come from camels, cows, or goats. Ethiopia's own variety of home-brewed beer is known as *tella* (TEH-lah), and can be made from barley, corn, or wheat. *Tej*, the Ethiopian wine, is made from honey and has been served in the country for centuries. It is usually poured from distinctive narrow-necked glass decanters.

Coffee has a long history in Ethiopia and is a favorite after-dinner beverage.

DINING OUT IN ADDIS ABABA

Addis Ababa's large population, international visitors, and cultural diversity feed a thriving restaurant industry. Besides traditional Ethiopian cuisine, one can find restaurants in the capital specializing in Italian, Indian, and Chinese food. Places to eat out range from street vendors and small snack bars to gourmet restaurants. Bakeries do a good business too. The international restaurants in the downtown area cater to the city's sizable affluent clientele seeking epicurean delights in stylish settings.

ETHIOPIA—HOME OF THE COFFEE BEAN

The word "coffee" is believed to have been derived from Kefa, the region in southwestern Ethiopia where coffee has been grown for centuries. In fact, legend has it that Ethiopia is the original home of the coffee bean.

Ethiopians enjoy coffee as much as Westerners do, but relatively few buy their coffee already processed. More often than not, rural Ethiopians roast their coffee beans themselves, grind them, and then pour hot water over the grounds. If they lack sugar, Ethiopians sometimes sweeten their coffee with honey. Coffee is the perfect beverage to round out an Ethiopian meal, particularly one with a spicy main dish. It is also a popular drink to serve guests.

Coffee is big business in Ethiopia. With about 300,000 tons of coffee produced annually, it is the country's number one export and often finds its way to specialty coffee shops in the United States. Commonly-exported Ethiopian coffees include the Sidamo, Yergacheffe, and Harer varieties.

TRADITIONS AND ETIQUETTE

The majority of Ethiopians living in the countryside do not have fixed mealtimes for breakfast, lunch, and dinner. Instead, they may have one or two hot meals per day and eat smaller portions of bread or dried meat as snacks. If breakfast is eaten, items served might include bread, hard-boiled or raw eggs, or porridge. Often only *injera* will be eaten in the morning. Ethiopians usually eat their main meal in the evening.

Sit-down meals often start with *tej* and bread. When the main course is served, Ethiopians do not usually use forks or spoons to eat. Instead they use *injera* to scoop up food and absorb the sauces. Letting one's fingers touch either the main dish, such as *wat*, or one's mouth while eating is considered bad manners.

Two teenage boys enjoying fresh milk. Milk is a popular beverage in Ethiopia.

ETHIOPIAN COFFEE CEREMONY

One of the most enjoyable experiences at an Ethiopian restaurant is the traditional coffee ceremony during which the coffee is taken through its complete life cycle of preparation in front of you.

The event usually starts with a woman bringing out washed coffee beans and roasting them in a roasting pan over a small open fire or coal furnace. The pan is not unlike an old-fashioned popcorn roasting pan. It has a long handle to keep the hand away from the heat, and the woman shakes the pan back and forth so that the beans will not burn. When the coffee beans start to pop, the woman will take

the roasted beans and walk around the room, filling the room with the smell of freshly roasted coffee.

The roasted coffee is then placed in a *mukecha* (moo-KE-ch-a), a heavy wooden bowl, and crushed by a wooden or metal stick known as a *zenezena* (zay-nay-zay-nah) in a rhythmic up and down fashion, much as how a pestle would be used to crush spices in a mortar. Most restaurants today use modern coffee grinders for this process. This is to save time, and the use of mechanical grinders does not take away much from the ceremony.

After crushing the roasted coffee beans into powder, it is put into a *jabena* (jay-BE-na), a traditional pot made out of clay. Water is added and the brew is boiled over an open fire or coal furnace. Once ready, the coffee aroma fills the room, and the coffee preparation process culminates in the guests sipping the first taste of coffee, served in small Chinese cups called *cini* (si-ni). Ethiopians usually stay for at least a second serving of coffee and sometimes a third.

Ethiopian restaurants have sprung up in many major U.S. cities, making Ethiopian food probably the most widely available type of African cuisine in the United States.

VEGETABLE *ALECHA* (VEGETABLE STEW)

1 cup bermuda onions
4 tablespoons oil
4 carrots, peeled and cut into 1-inch slices
4 potatoes, cut into thick slices
2 tomatoes, blanched in boiling water, skins removed, and cut into 16 wedges
12-ounce (340-gram) can tomato sauce
3 cups water
8 cabbage wedges, 1-inch wide
4 green peppers, cleaned and quartered
Salt
Pepper
½ teaspoon ground ginger

In a 4-quart saucepan, sauté onions in oil until they are soft but not brown. Add the carrots and cook for 10 minutes covered. Add potatoes, peeled tomatoes, tomato sauce, and water. Cover the saucepan and cook for 10 minutes. Add cabbage wedges and green peppers. Sprinkle with salt, pepper, and ground ginger. Cook until vegetables are tender. Season as required. Serve in an attractive bowl.

DABO KOLO (ROASTED COOKIES)

2 cups all-purpose flour
½ teaspoon salt
2 tablespoons sugar
½ teaspoon cayenne pepper
¼ cup oil

In a 1-quart bowl, mix all-purpose flour, salt, sugar, cayenne pepper, and oil. Knead ingredients together and add water, spoonful by spoonful, to form stiff dough. Knead the dough for an additional five minutes. Tear off a piece of dough the size of a golf ball. Roll it out with palms of hands on a lightly-floured board into a long strip, ½ inch thick. Form with cookie cutter into rounds 2½ inches in diameter with scissors. Spread enough pieces to cover the bottom of a ungreased 9-inch frying pan. Cook over heat until uniformly light brown on all sides. Continue until all pieces are fried.

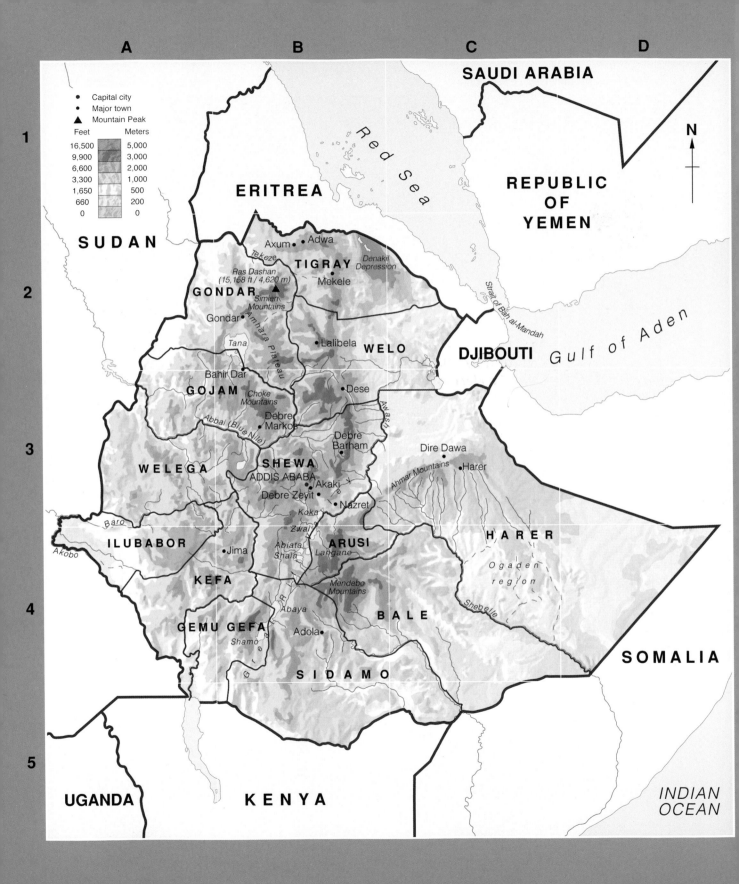

	A	B	C	D

1

SAUDI ARABIA

Red Sea

REPUBLIC OF YEMEN

N

- Capital city
- Major town
- ▲ Mountain Peak

Feet	Meters
16,500	5,000
9,900	3,000
6,600	2,000
3,300	1,000
1,650	500
660	200
0	0

SUDAN

ERITREA

Axum • • Adwa

Tekeze

TIGRAY

Denakil Depression

Ras Dashan
(15,168 ft / 4,620 m) ▲

Simien Mountains

GONDAR

• Mekele

2

Gondar •

Amhara Plateau

Tana

• Lalibela

WELO

DJIBOUTI

Strait of Bab al-Mandah

Gulf of Aden

Bahir Dar •

GOJAM

Choke Mountains

• Dese

Awash

Abbai (Blue Nile)

Debre Markos •

Debre Barham •

Dire Dawa •

3

WELEGA

SHEWA

ADDIS ABABA

• Akaki

Debre Zeyit •

Koka

• Nazret

Ahmar Mountains

• Harer

HARER

Ogaden region

Baro

Zwai

Akobo

ILUBABOR

• Jima

Abiata
Shala

Langane

ARUSI

Shebelle

KEFA

Mendebo Mountains

4

Abaya

BALE

GEMU GEFA

• Adola

SOMALIA

Shamo

Green R.

SIDAMO

5

UGANDA

KENYA

INDIAN OCEAN

MAP OF ETHIOPIA

Abbai River, A3, B3
Abaya Lake, B4
Abiata Lake, B4
Addis Ababa, B3
Adola, B4
Adwa, B2
Ahmar Mountains, C3
Akaki, B3
Akobo River, A4
Amhara Plateau, B2
Arusi Province, B3–B4, C4
Awash River, B3
Axum, B2

Bahir Dar, B2–B3
Bale Province, B4, C4–C5
Baro River, A3

Choke Mountains, B3

Debre Barham, B3
Debre Markos, B3
Debre Zeyit, B3
Denakil Depression, B2
Dese, B3
Dire Dawa, C3
Djibouti, C2–C3

Eritrea, A1–A2, B1–B2, C2

Gemu Gefa Province, A4–A5, B4–B5
Gojam Province, A2–A3, B2–B3
Gondar City, B2
Gondar Province, A2, B2–B3
Great Rift Valley B4
Gulf of Aden, C2–C3, D2–D3

Harer City, C3
Harer Province, B3–B4, C3–C4, D3–D4

Ilubabor Province, A3–A4, B3–B4
Indian Ocean, D4–D5

Jima, B4

Kefa Province, A3–A4, B3–B4
Kenya, A5, B5, C5
Koka Lake, B3

Lalibela, B2
Langano Lake, B4

Mekele, B2
Mendebo Mountains, B4

Nazret, B3

Ogaden region, C4

Ras Dashan, B2
Red Sea, B1–B2, C1–C2
Republic of Yemen, C1–C2, D1–D2

Saudi Arabia, C1, D1
Shala Lake, B4
Shamo Lake, B4
Shebelle River, C4
Shewa Province, B3–B4
Sidamo Province, B4–B5, C4–C5

Simien Mountains, B2
Somalia, C3–C5, D3–D5
Strait of Bah al-Mandah, C2
Sudan, A1–A5, B1

Tana Lake, B2
Tekeze River, B2
Tigray Province, B2, C2

Uganda, A5

Welega Province, A3, B3
Welo Province, B2–B3, C2–C3

Zwai Lake, B4

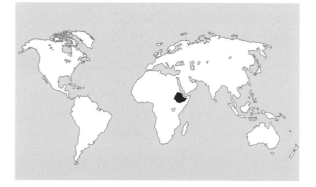

ECONOMIC ETHIOPIA

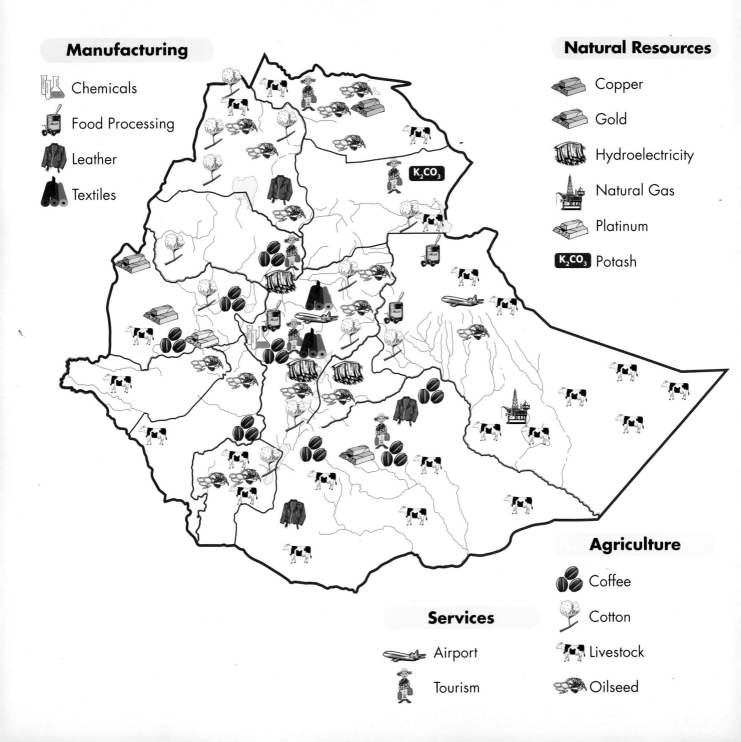

Manufacturing
- Chemicals
- Food Processing
- Leather
- Textiles

Natural Resources
- Copper
- Gold
- Hydroelectricity
- Natural Gas
- Platinum
- K_2CO_3 Potash

Services
- Airport
- Tourism

Agriculture
- Coffee
- Cotton
- Livestock
- Oilseed

ABOUT THE ECONOMY

OVERVIEW
Under the new government, Ethiopia has moved from a centrally planned economy to a market oriented one, boosting its GDP growth rate from 2.8 percent under the Derg (1974–91) to 6.5 percent in 2005. Its economy is largely based on agriculture, which accounts for half of its GDP and 80 percent of its employment. Coffee is Ethiopia's major export. One of the world's poorest countries, Ethiopia's economy suffers from problems such as a burgeoning population, large-scale environmental degradation, soil exhaustion, and inefficient rural land-holding policies.

GROSS DOMESTIC PRODUCT
$60.34 billion (2005 estimate)

GROWTH RATE
8.9 percent (2005 estimate)

INFLATION RATE
6 percent (2005 estimate)

EXTERNAL DEBT
$5.1 billion (2005 estimate)

CURRENCY
1 Ethiopian birr (ETB) = 100 cents
Notes: 1; 5; 10; 50; 100 birr
Coins: 1; 5; 10; 25; 50
USD 1= 8.72 ETB (October 2006)

LAND USE
Arable land 10.01 percent, permanent crops 0.65 percent, other 89.34 percent (2005 estimates)

NATURAL RESOURCES
Small reserves of gold, platinum, copper, potash, natural gas, hydroelectricity

AGRICULTURAL PRODUCTS
Cereals, pulses, coffee, oilseed, cotton, sugarcane, potatoes, qat, cut flowers, hides, cattle, sheep, goats, fish

INDUSTRIAL PRODUCTS
Food processing, beverages, textiles, leather, chemicals, metals processing, cement

MAJOR EXPORTS
Coffee, qat, gold, leather products, oilseed

MAJOR IMPORTS
Food and live animals, petroleum and petroleum products, chemicals, machinery, motor vehicles, cereals, textiles

MAJOR IMPORT PARTNERS
Saudi Arabia 25.3 percent, United States 15.8 percent, China 6.6 percent (2004 estimates)

MAJOR EXPORT PARTNERS
Djibouti 13.3 percent, Germany 10 percent, Japan 8.4 percent, Saudi Arabia 5.6 percent, United States 5.2 percent, United Arab Emirates 5 percent, Italy 4.6 percent (2004 estimates)

CULTURAL ETHIOPIA

Castles of Gondar
Gondar was once the capital of Ethiopia (1632–1868) and during this period, various kings built castles and fortress-like battlements, making Gondar home to many fascinating ancient ruins.

Axum
Carved obelisks from single blocks of granite, with one standing at 75.4 feet (23 m), and many other remarkable monuments are located in Ethiopia's holiest city.

Simien Mountains National Park
Renowned for its dramatic topography due to the erosion around basalt lavas, scenery, excellent hiking, and endemic wildlife, this park is popular with nature lovers and hikers.

Churches of Lalibela
This is the site of 11 ancient rock churches that have been hewn from bedrock and are distinctive in architecture and design.

Blue Nile Falls
A waterfall of great natural beauty, the Blue Nile Falls is estimated to be 121 to 147.6 feet (37 to 45 m) high and is only 18.6 miles (30 km) away from the town of Bahir Dar.

Addis Ababa
The capital, which is an important diplomatic center for the African continent, thrives with exciting cultural diversity. Places of interest include the university, Saint George's Cathedral, the Menelik Mausoleum, and the Merkato.

Great Rift Valley Lakes
The seven lakes of the Great Rift Valley offer ideal bird-watching and wildlife-viewing opportunities. Of the seven lakes, Lagano, Abiata, and Shala are the most popular.

Sof Omar Cave
Formed by the Weyb River, this 10-mile (16-km) cave system can be explored by foot. Tall pillars of stone 65.6 feet (20 m) high and fluted archways make this natural phenomeno a must-see for visitors.

ABOUT THE CULTURE

OFFICIAL NAME
Ityop'iya Federalawi Demokrasiyawi Ripeblik
(Federal Democratic Republic of Ethiopia)

NATIONAL FLAG
Three equal horizontal bands of green, yellow, and red with a yellow pentagram and single yellow rays emanating from the angles between the points on a light blue disk centered on the three bands

CAPITAL
Addis Ababa

AREA
435,186 square miles (1.13 million sq km)

POPULATION
74,777,981 (2006 estimate)

BIRTH RATE
37.98 births per 1,000 Ethiopians (2006 estimate)

DEATH RATE
14.86 deaths per 1000 Ethiopians (2006 estimate)

AGE STRUCTURE
0–14 years: 43.7 percent; 15–64 years: 53.6 percent; 65 years and over: 2.7 percent

ETHNIC GROUPS
Oromo 40 percent, Amhara and Tigre 32 percent, Sidamo 9 percent, Shankella 6 percent, Somali 6 percent, Afar 4 percent, Gurage 2 percent, other 1 percent (1999 estimates)

MAJOR RELIGIONS
Muslim 45–50 percent, Ethiopian Orthodox 35–40 percent, traditional faiths 12 percent, other faiths 3–8 percent

MAIN LANGUAGES
Amharic, Tigrinya, Oromigna, Guaragigna, Somali, Arabic, other local languages, English (mainly taught in schools)

LITERACY RATE
Ethiopians aged 15 and above who can both read and write: 42.7 percent (2003 estimate)

IMPORTANT ANNIVERSARIES
Ethiopian Patriots Day (April 6), Victory of Adwa commemoration (March 2), National Day (May 28)

LEADERS IN POLITICS
Haile Selassie, emperor (1930–74)
Mengistu Haile Mariam, leader of military
    government (1977–91)
Girma Wolde Giorgis, president since 2001
Meles Zenawi, prime minister since 1995

TIME LINE

IN ETHIOPIA	IN THE WORLD

5000 B.C.
Hunters and gatherers settle in the Ethiopian highlands.

753 B.C.
Rome is founded.

116–17 B.C.
The Roman empire reaches its greatest extent, under Emperor Trajan (98–17 B.C.).

A.D. 200
Migrants from Arabia mix with the local population to establish the kingdom of Axum, which becomes a thriving trading center.

A.D. 600
Height of Mayan civilization

1000
The Chinese perfect gunpowder and begin to use it in warfare.

1100–1200
The Zagwe dynasty of monarchs rules over an era of great artistic achievements.

1270
The Solomonic dynasty is restored. The Amharic language and Orthodox Christianity spread throughout the Ethiopian highlands.

1530
Beginning of transatlantic slave trade organized by the Portuguese in Africa.

1558–1603
Reign of Elizabeth I of England

1620
Pilgrims sail the *Mayflower* to America.

1776
U.S. Declaration of Independence

1789–99
The French Revolution

1861
The U.S. Civil War begins.

1869
The Suez Canal is opened.

1889
Addis Ababa becomes Ethiopia's capital.

1896
Italy invades Ethiopia but is defeated by the Ethiopians at the battle of Adwa.

1914
World War I begins.

1930
Emperor Haile Selassie I assumes the throne.

IN ETHIOPIA	IN THE WORLD
1936 Emperor Selassie flees Ethiopia when Addis Ababa falls to the invading Italians. Ethiopia becomes part of Italian East Africa.	
	1939 World War II begins.
1941 Selassie is restored to the throne when British troops defeat the Italians.	
1941–60 Selassie implements a series of important educational, political, and economic reforms.	**1945** The United States drops atomic bombs on Hiroshima and Nagasaki. **1949** The North Atlantic Treaty Organization (NATO) is formed. **1957** The Russians launch Sputnik.
1962 Selassie annexes Eritrea, triggering the start of Africa's longest war.	**1966–69** The Chinese Cultural Revolution
1971–74 Selassie is overthrown and the monarchy is replaced by a Socialist military government.	
1977–78 Mengistu Haile Mariam comes into power and launches the "Red Terror" campaign, which results in the deaths of 100,000 Ethiopians.	
1983–85 A huge famine claims at least 300,000 lives.	
	1986 Nuclear disaster at Chernobyl in Ukraine
1991 The Ethiopian People's Revolutionary Democratic Front captures Addis Ababa. Meles Zenawi becomes the interim president.	**1991** Breakup of the Soviet Union
1993 Eritrea gains independence from Ethiopia.	
	1997 Hong Kong is returned to China.
1999–2002 War with Eritrea	**2001** Terrorists crash planes in New York, Washington, D.C., and Pennsylvania.
2005 Protests erupt over alleged electoral fraud.	**2003** War in Iraq

GLOSSARY

Abun (AH-boon)
Official head of the Ethiopian Orthodox Church.

berbere (ber-BER-ray)
A spice mixture that is added to many traditional Ethiopian dishes.

bereha (ber-eh-HAH)
The semidesert region, including the Denakil Depression and other low-lying areas.

dega (DEH-ga)
The cool region, chiefly the Amhara Plateau.

Derg (durg)
The military government that ruled Ethiopia from 1974 to 1991. It came under the leadership of Mengistu Haile Mariam in 1977. Derg literally means "committee" in Amharic.

Enkutatash (en-koo-TAH-tahsh)
Literally "gift of jewels," the name for the Ethiopian New Year's Day.

Ganna (gehn-NAH)
Ethiopian Christmas.

injera (in-JAIR-ah)
A flat bread made from teff flour.

jabena (jay-BE-na)
A traditional pot made of clay.

k'amis (kah-MEES)
A white cotton gown that women sometimes wear underneath the *shamma*.

kolla (KOH-la)
The hot region, including eastern Ogaden, the valleys of the Blue Nile and Tekeze rivers, and areas along the Kenyan and Sudanese borders.

kur (kuhr)
The alpine region, including the highest elevations in Ethiopia.

Merkato (mer-KAH-toe)
The large, open-air market in Addis Ababa. Attracts Ethiopians from all over the country.

mesob (meh-SOHB)
A large basket used as a table.

mukecha (moo-KE- ch-a)
A heavy wooden bowl.

shamma (SHEH-mah)
A one-piece cotton wrap worn over the shoulders and arms.

teff
A grain that is indigenous to Ethiopia.

Timkat (TIM-keht)
Epiphany, the most important religious festival in Ethiopia.

wat (weht)
A highly spiced stew that is eaten with *injera*.

weina dega (WAY-nuh DEH-ga)
The temperate region, including the lower regions of the Amhara and Somali plateaus.

FURTHER INFORMATION

BOOKS

Beckwith, Carol and Angela Fisher. *African Ark: The Peoples and Ancient Cultures of Ethiopia and the Horn of Africa.* New York: Harry N. Abrams, 1990.

Gilkes, Patrick. *Conflict in Somalia and Ethiopia.* New York: New Discovery Books, 1994.

Hall, John G. *Ethiopia in the Modern World.* Philadelphia, PA: Chelsea House Publishers, 2003.

Marcus, Harold G. *A History of Ethiopia* (Updated Edition). Berkeley, CA: University of California Press, 2002.

Parker, Ben. *Ethiopia: Breaking New Ground.* Oxford: Oxfam, 1995.

Waugh, Evelyn. *The Coronation of Haile Selassie.* London: Penguin, 2005.

Zuehlke, Jeffrey. *Ethiopia in Pictures.* Minneapolis, MN: Lerner Publications, 2005.

WEB SITES

An Alternative Source of Ethiopian News and Views. www.ethiomedia.com

Central Intelligence Agency World Factbook (select Ethiopia from list of countries). www.cia.gov/cia/publications/factbook

Lonely Planet World Guide: Ethiopia. www.lonelyplanet.com/worldguide/destinations/africa/ethiopia/

Portals to the World: Ethiopia. www.loc.gov/rr/international/amed/ethiopia/ethiopia.html

The Addis Tribune www.addistribune.com

VIDEOS

Africa's Child: Ethiopia—Festival of Fire. Channel 4, 2000.

Ethiopia. Pilot Productions, 1997.

MUSIC

Addis Live! Ethiopian Music and Entertainment. www.addislive.com

Gigi. Gigi. Palm Pictures (Audio), 2000.

Tesfaye: A Future Hope: Vocal and String Music of Ethiopia. Seleshe Damessae. Music of the World, 1994.

The Rough Guide to the Music of Ethiopia. Varous artists. World Music Network, 2004.

BIBLIOGRAPHY

Beckwith, Carol and Angela Fisher. *African Ark: People and Ancient Cultures of Ethiopia and the Horn of Africa.* New York: Harry N. Abrams, 1990.

Brown, Judith R. *Farnji: A Venture into Ethiopia.* Santa Barbara, CA: Fithian Press, 1994.

Endeshaw, Assafa. *Ethiopia: Perspectives for Change and Renewal.* Singapore: Seng Lee Press Pvt. Ltd., 2002.

Gilkes, Patrick. *Conflict in Somalia and Ethiopia.* New York: New Discovery Books, 1994.

Kurtz, Jane. *Ethiopia: The Roof of Africa.* New York: Dillon Press, 1991.

Ofcansky, Thomas. *Ethiopia: A Country Study.* Washington, D.C: U.S. Government Printing Office, 1992.

Shelemay, Kay K. *A Song of Longing: An Ethiopian Journey.* Champaign, IL: University of Illinois Press, 1992.

Stewart, Gail B. *Ethiopia.* New York: Crestwood House, 1991.

Central Statistical Agency of Ethiopia. www.csa.gov.et

Ministry of Foreign Affairs of Ethiopia. www.mfa.gov.et

Ministry of Information of Ethiopia. www.moinfo.gov.et

INDEX

African Ark, 67, 83

African, Caribbean, and Pacific Group of States, 34

African Union, 14, 23, 34, 96

agriculture, 5, 9, 11, 12, 25, 37, 38, 39, 41, 46, 56, 58, 63, 67, 68, 70, 99, 122, 123

   coffee beans, 13, 38, 39, 56, 127, 129

   collective farms, 25, 68

   enset, 56

   irrigation, 9

   land redistribution, 68

   teff, 12, 39, 56, 91, 123

   tobacco, 39, 40, 56

Algeria, 24

Amhara National Democratic Movement, 30

Andom, Aman, 25

Arabia, 18, 81, 90

Arabian Peninsula, 7, 81

azmari, 102

Badme, 24

battles and wars,

   Battle of Adwa, 15, 20, 22

   Eritrean-Ethiopian War, 24

   war on terror, 34

   World War II, 24

Blue Nile Falls, 43, 45

buna bet, 105

Burundi, 34, 35

circumcision, 63

Commission for Africa, 15, 34

Congo, the, 34

constitution, 5, 23, 25, 27, 29, 50, 71
coups d'état, 5, 23

deforestation, 41, 45
Denakil Depression, 7, 9, 10, 11, 12, 109
Denakil Desert, 13, 48
Derg, the, 25, 29, 35, 37, 50
desertification, 45, 46
Desta, Gebre Kristos, 98
diseases, 54, 69, 74, 75
    HIV/AIDS, 74–75
    malaria, 74
Djibouti, 7, 35, 42, 72, 106
droughts, 12, 37, 39, 105, 121
dulas, 59
dynasties, 19, 20, 21, 88
    Solomonic, 19, 20, 88
    Zagwe, 19, 20, 21

economy, 22, 23, 25, 26, 27, 37, 38, 39, 40, 42, 61, 69, 71, 72, 73, 74, 78
    energy resources, 41
    gross domestic product (GDP), 32, 37, 38, 40
    handicrafts, 99, 100
    industry, 40, 43, 58, 71, 99
    leather goods, 39, 40, 100
    market economy, 37
    mining, 40–41
    privatization, 37
    tourism, 43, 49, 102
education, 37, 56, 61, 70, 71–74, 72, 73, 74, 75, 77, 89, 98
    Addis Ababa University, 73
    University School of Fine Art and Design, 98, 99
Egypt, 15, 19, 77, 80, 106
elections, 23, 27, 29, 30, 31, 33
Emperor Constantine, 78, 117
Eritrea, 7, 22, 24, 26, 27, 31, 32, 35, 57
Eritrean Liberation Front, 24
Ethiopian Human Rights Council (EHRCO), 33
Ethiopian National Defence Force (ENDF), 32
Ethiopian People's Revolutionary Democratic Front (EPRDF), 26, 27, 29, 30, 31, 43, 53
ethnic groups
    Afar, 57, 81, 83, 100, 109
    Amharas, 53, 55, 56, 58, 59, 67, 78, 85

Anuak, 33, 57
Berta, 57, 88
Falashas, 85, 93
Gumuz, 57
Gurage, 57, 83
Hareri, 83
Kunama, 57, 88
Nara, 57
Nuer, 57
Oromos, 53, 55, 59, 63, 83, 92, 100
Shankella, 57
Sidama, 56, 57, 83
Somalis, 33, 53, 57, 82, 83, 97, 103
Surma, 67, 101, 110, 111
Tigrayans, 30, 53, 55, 56, 59, 78, 92
tribal peoples, 48, 101, 103

famines, 5, 7, 13, 22, 25, 26, 39, 48, 61, 85, 105, 121
Federal Democratic Republic of Ethiopia (FDRE), 5, 27, 29, 88
food and beverages
    berbere, 121, 123, 124, 125
    coffee, 126, 127, 129
        cini, 129
        coffee ceremony, 129
        jabena, 129
        mukecha, 129
        zenezena, 129
    dabo kolo, 125
    injera, 12, 122, 123, 124, 128
    kitfo, 124
    milk, 126, 128
    niter kebbeh, 125
    tej, 126
    tella, 126
    wat, 121, 123, 124, 125, 128
    yataklete kilkil, 124
    yemiser selatta, 124
    yeshimbra assa, 125
France, 21, 22

Gabre-Medhin, Tsegaye, 96
Gaysay Valley, 51
Gebreselassie, Haile, 105, 108
Gigi, 103
Giorgis, Girma Wolde, 29
gorges, 7, 9, 43
    Blue Nile Gorge, 43
Great Britain, 21, 22, 34
Great Rift Valley, 7, 8, 9, 12, 13, 43, 45
Greece, 5, 15

Hagos, Desta, 98, 99
health care, 37, 54, 71, 74, 75
Horn of Africa, 7, 34, 89
human rights and press freedom, 25, 33, 34, 35, 68
Human Rights League, 33

Indian Ocean, 7
infant mortality rate, 54, 62
International Monetary Fund, 34, 37
Italian occupation, 22–23
Italy, 15, 21, 22, 23, 40, 106

Jerusalem, 19, 85

Kenya, 7, 107
Kibre Negest, 20, 89
Kosrof, Wosene Worke, 98

languages
    Afro-Asiatic, 57, 87
    Amharic, 18, 20, 23, 25, 45, 55, 56, 87, 88, 89, 90, 91, 92, 93, 97
    Ge'ez, 18, 85, 87, 88, 89, 90, 95
    Himyaritic alphabet, 90
    Nilo-Saharan, 57, 87, 88
    Oromo, 87, 91, 92, 93
    Somali, 87, 92
    Tigrinya, 56, 87, 90, 92
League of Nations, 22
legso, 66
Liberia, 17, 34, 35
life expectancy, 54, 74
literacy rate, 71

Mariam, Mengistu Haile, 26, 27, 30, 31, 35, 37, 43, 50, 51, 53, 58, 68, 71, 72, 79, 82, 92, 105
maps
    cultural Ethiopia, 136
    economic Ethiopia, 134
    map of Ethiopia, 132
monarchs, 14, 19, 21, 29, 78, 88, 89, 106, 117
    Asmara, 21
    Ezanas, 19
    Haile Selassie I, 17, 19, 22, 22–25, 23, 24, 25, 30, 34, 73, 78, 82, 88, 97, 106, 107
    King Solomon, 19, 97, 116
    Menelik II, 15, 21, 23, 88
    Queen of Sheba, 19, 97, 116
    Tewodros II, 21, 88
    Yohannis IV, 21

mountains and mountain ranges, 8, 9,
    11, 12, 13, 43, 47, 48, 49, 51, 83, 84,
    101, 114
    Ahmar, 9
    Arusi, 48
    Bale, 47, 48, 49, 83
    Gaysay, 51
    Imet Gogo, 8
    Mendebo, 9
    Simien, 8, 13, 43, 47, 48, 49

Nubia, 15

Ogaden National Liberation Front, 30
Olympics, the, 107, 108
Oromo Liberation Front, 30
Oromo People's Democratic Organization,
    30
overcultivation, 45
overgrazing, 39, 45, 47
overpopulation, 37, 45

parliament, 25, 29, 31
Portugal, 20, 21

qire (iddir), 67
Queen Taytu, 15

recipes
    Dabo kolo (roasted cookies), 131
    Vegetable alecha (vegetable stew),
        130
Red Sea, 18, 57, 83
Red Terror, the, 26, 50
regions, 7, 8, 10, 12, 19, 33, 41, 43, 45,
    57, 61, 66, 68, 81, 93, 100, 101, 103,
    117, 118, 127
    Afar, 92
    Anuak, 33, 57
    Bale, 100
    Denakil, 81
    Gambella, 33
    Illubabor, 41
    Kefa, 41, 87, 127
    Ogaden, 7, 11, 12, 26, 57, 103
    Oromo, 91, 92, 93, 100
    Shakiso, 41
    Shewa, 30, 41, 57
    Somali, 92
    Tigray, 19, 25, 26, 30, 41, 92
    Welega, 41
    Welo, 25

religions
    animism and traditional beliefs, 55, 56,
        77, 83, 84, 96, 113
        adbar, 84
        buda, 84
    Coptic Church of Egypt, 19, 77, 80
    Ethiopian Orthodox Church, 19, 20,
        55, 56, 62, 77, 78, 79, 80, 89, 95,
        100, 102, 113, 115, 116
        Abun, 80, 116
        Ark of the Covenant, 14, 115
        Church of Bet Giyorgis, 79
        Church of the Nativity, 113
        clergy, 78, 79, 80, 84
        debtera, 80, 84
        Episcopal Synod, 80
        Giorgis Cathedral, 15
        parishes, 78
        patron saints, 79, 97, 102, 117,
            118
        Saint George's Cathedral, 15
        Saint Mary of Zion Church, 14,
            15
        tabot, 115
        Trinity Cathedral, 114
    Islam, 20, 21, 55, 56, 57, 59, 64, 65,
        67, 77, 80, 80–81, 81, 82, 83, 84,
        95, 100, 113, 119
        Koran, 81
        Prophet Muhammad, 81, 83, 114
        Ramadan, 81, 113, 114, 119
        shahada, 81
        Sheikh Hussein, 83
        Shia, 83
        Sunni, 83
    Judaism, 19, 20, 85
    Western Christianity, 78
        European missionaries, 17, 61, 77,
            78
        Protestants, 80
        Roman Catholicism, 21
rivers, 9, 10, 11, 13, 17, 18, 42, 45, 49,
    101
    Awash, 9, 10, 17, 49
    Baro, 9, 10
    Blue Nile (Abbai), 9, 11
    Shebelle, 9
    Tekeze, 9, 11
Rwanda, 34

Socialism, 24, 25, 29, 73, 96
soil erosion, 39, 45, 46, 47
Somalia, 7, 35, 57, 72
Soviet Union, 26, 27, 105

Sudan, 7, 9, 18, 22, 35, 41, 42, 57, 72,
    85, 88, 106

Tekle, Afewerk, 15, 97, 98
towns and cities
    Addis Ababa, 10, 14, 15, 22, 23, 27,
        29, 31, 32, 34, 38, 40, 42, 43, 49,
        69, 71, 72, 73, 80, 89, 92, 96, 97,
        98, 105, 106, 107, 113, 114, 115,
        116, 117, 122, 124, 127
    Aramis, 17
    Aseb, 21
    Awassa, 14
    Axum, 14, 15, 18, 19, 20, 43, 56,
        65, 77, 80, 85, 96, 100
    Bahir Dar, 14, 32, 40, 43, 58
    Debre Markos, 14
    Debre Sina, 113
    Debre Zeyit, 32
    Dessie, 14
    Dinsho, 51
    Dire Dawa, 14, 18, 29, 32, 40, 42,
        118
    Entoto, 15
    Gondar, 15, 32, 43, 77, 85, 100,
        117
    Gonder, 14
    Gore, 32
    Harer, 81, 84, 100
    Harrar, 14
    Jijiga, 32
    Jimma, 14
    Lalibela, 43, 77, 79, 100, 103
    Massawa, 21
    Mekele, 14
    Nazareth, 14
    Nekemite, 14

UNESCO, 17, 71
United Ethiopian Democratic Forces
    (UEDF), 30
United Nations, 14, 15, 24, 32, 34, 35,
    39, 46, 74
United Nations Children's Fund (UNICEF),
    14
United States, 17, 33, 34, 72, 74, 129

World Education Forum, 73
World Health Organization (WHO), 14
World Trade Organization, 34

Zenawi, Meles, 27, 30, 34, 51, 92
Zimbabwe, 27, 35